Employment Counselling Theory and Strategies:
A Book of Readings

edited by

Norman E. Amundson
Gray Poehnell
Stuart Smithson

in association with
Human Resources Development Canada

Ergon Communications
Richmond, British Columbia

Canadian Cataloguing in Publication Data

Employment counselling theory and strategies: a book of readings.

Includes bibliographical references
ISBN 0-660-16866-9   Catalogue Number MP43-368/1997E

1. Vocational guidance. 2. Vocational guidance – Psychological aspects.
3. Career changes. 4. Counselling.   I. Amundson, Norman E. (Norman
Edmund), 1948-   . II. Poehnell, Gray. III. Smithson, Stuart. IV.
Canada. Human Resources Development Canada.

HF5381.E56 1997   331.7'02
C97-980053-6

Published by Ergon Communications in association with Human
Resources Development Canada, Human Resources Investment
Directorate.

Orders and inquiries to:

Ergon
Communications
3260 Springford Ave., Richmond, B.C. V7E 1T9 Canada
Fax: (604) 448-9025

Printed in Canada by Hignell Book Printing,
488 Burnell Street, Winnipeg, Manitoba, R3G 2B4; Tel. 204 784-1033

Acknowledgements

This book of readings could not have been completed without the active support and participation of a number of people. Special thanks to:

- Celine Renaud, Michel Turcotte, Cheri Crosby from NHQ for their direct support of necessary resources and the less tangible support of encouragement.
- Janet Hollingsworth from NHQ, who worked out the evaluation requirements for the revised Individual Employment Counselling training program for HRDC and shared her knowledge freely with the trainers and the participants.
- Charles Perrin, the Manager of Employment Programs and Services, BC/YT Region for his generous contribution of our Region's resources.
- Jeanette Amundson, Nora Lowe and Valerie Thiessen for their assistance in proof-reading the manuscript.
- Dr. Robert Drummond, editor of the Journal of Employment Counseling, for his support and encouragement.
- All the authors of the original articles for allowing us to edit and include their works in this volume.

Table of Contents

List of Figures

Introduction

Norman E. Amundson, Gray Poehnell, and Stuart Smithson

Individual employment counselling training within Human Resources Development Canada (HRDC) has been well served by the text developed by Bezanson, DeCoff and Stewart (1985) and the Systematic Counselling model. As with all counselling theory, however, times change and new models emerge for consideration. This current book of readings is designed to build on the ideas of the past and to present some current articles which provide background for the recently developed Career Pathways exploration workbook (Amundson and Poehnell, 1995) and the recently revised individual employment counselling training program for HRDC (Amundson, Smithson, Thiessen and Poehnell, 1996). The theories and counselling strategies presented here have application beyond HRDC and can be easily adapted to other career counselling contexts.

One of the difficulties in putting together a book of readings is developing a sense of coherence with the material involved. To facilitate the flow of ideas, some adaptations have been made. Relevant information from the Bezanson, DeCoff and Stewart (1985) text has been summarized and included where appropriate. Some changes have also been made to the other material to allow greater consistency. Also after each of the readings in the text, a series of questions have been put forward for study purposes. These questions help focus attention on the major themes of the articles.

Three general sections have been used to help organize the book. The first section focuses on some foundational concepts which underlie the employment counselling process. The opening article in this section provides a broad interactional perspective on decision making. The model presented here lays a framework for how people perceive situations and the role of the counsellor within the reframing process. From this overarching model, the focus shifts to more personal issues. "Negotiating Identity" reflects the interactional nature of identity development and the need to re-negotiate a personal sense of identity in the face of unemployment. The emotional reactions (an emotional rollercoaster) which play a part in this negotiation process are highlighted in the next article, the "Dynamics of Unemployment." Coming to terms with the stress and challenge of unemployment depends in large measure on the creation of a positive counselling climate. The article on "Mattering" describes how counsellors can help clients feel that they have significance (they matter) despite their change of circumstances. Within this context, it is not surprising that clients and counsellors face some difficult situations. The concluding article on "Client Reluctance" helps put this into perspective and offers some practical suggestions for coping with challenging clients.

In section two, the focus shifts from foundational concepts to the formulation of an overall career counselling plan. It is at this point that counsellors consider the system that they will be using in their counselling practice. The opening article lays out a "Centric Model" which includes four broad phases of development. This model is consistent with the Relating/Investigating/Synthesizing/Consolidating (RISC) counselling approach used in the revised individual employment counselling training. A spin-off from this model is the second article which addresses "Action Planning Through the Phases of Counselling." The position put forward here is that both clients and counsellors must be regarded as active agents through all the phases of counselling. Following the two articles on the general model of counselling, there is an article which addresses the connecting point between an initial assessment interview and the employment counselling which follows. This connection is characterized by an invitation to "Refocus on the Assessment Goal." Counselling is certainly not a linear process and there is often a need to change directions and to reconceptualize the counselling plan. The article addressing "Metaphors and Drawings in Case Conceptualization" is designed to focus attention on the change process using visual imagery. The concluding article in this section provides several "Perspectives for Assessing Career Development." As counsellors seek to develop an appropriate counselling plan, they need to keep in mind how their particular perspective influences the counselling process and communication between other professionals and their clients. This awareness of perspective has implications for counselling with individuals as well as for general program development and assessment.

Moving beyond the general counselling plan to the next section, there is a need to focus attention on specific counselling strategies. The opening article in this third section illustrates several counselling strategies for working with cross cultural clients. Particular emphasis is placed on the notions of bridging, transferable skills and attitudes and behavior rehearsal. While these techniques have particular relevance within a cross cultural context, they are also important skills when working with any client. The second article in this series, "Supporting Clients Through a Change in Perspective," briefly illustrates twelve reframing strategies and organizes these approaches using the dimension of time (i.e., looking back, the present, looking ahead). Keeping within the theme of "reframing," the article, "Myths, Metaphors and Moxie," addresses how reframing can proceed at several different levels with respect to beliefs, images and action. The next article, the "Pattern Identification Exercise," illustrates a comprehensive method for exploring career themes using contrasting experiences as the method of inquiry. This process of analysis generates some interesting information while teaching a procedure for ongoing exploration of experiences. Moving beyond an exploration phase, the next two articles address "Cognitive Decision Making" and a "Learning Strategy." The decision-making article relies primarily on a cognitive model of assessment. For more intuitive decision-making methods, the reader is referred back to some of the intuitive approaches presented by H.B. Gelatt in the Fundamentals course (i.e., positive uncertainty). The learning article describes the counselling strategies of observation, rehearsal, feedback and systematic learning. The article on "Self Management" builds upon the learning theme but shifts the focus to how clients can assume more responsibility for their own progress. This perspective puts into practice some of the notions that were expressed earlier about the importance of regarding clients and counsellors as active agents in the action planning process. The concluding article in this section presents some ideas on the strategies and issues which need to be taken into account during the "Termination Phase of Counselling." The focus here includes follow-up with clients, record keeping, evaluation and self reflection. Following this, there is a brief postscript on the need for further development and training for the employment counsellor. Maintaining an active learning approach is highlighted as a critical component in the current market place.

Employment Counselling

Theory and Strategies

PART ONE

Foundational Concepts

1

An Interactive Model
of Career Decision Making

Norman E. Amundson

Career decision making is something that occurs throughout life as people seek to manoeuvre through education, work, and other life experiences. The necessity of making good career decisions is particularly important in the current context of economic and social change. To understand fully the career decision making process requires not only an awareness of rational decision making techniques, but also an appreciation of how people come to form perceptions (determining contexts), what determines the need for a decision (decision triggers), how decisions are framed and reframed, and how decisions are implemented (action). The need for a broadly based understanding of decision making has been well articulated by Gelatt (1989) and others.

The purpose of this paper is to outline a model of career decision making which illustrates the interactional nature of the decision making process. Approaching decision making from this perspective has implications for the practice of employment counselling.

This chapter is an adapted version of Amundson, N.E. (1995a). An interactive model of career decision making. *Journal of Employment Counseling*, 32, 11-21. Used by permission.

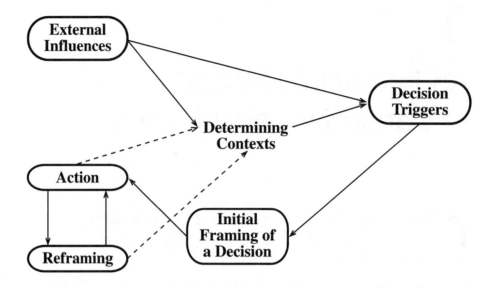

Figure 1.1
The Interactive Decision Making Process

Components of the Interactive Career Decision Making Model

Determining Contexts

The way in which we make decisions is heavily influenced by factors such as our culture, economic and political events, the interpersonal roles that we have assumed throughout life, and our basic self structure. These environmental and personal factors help determine our perceptions and ultimately the decisions we make (Rogoff & Lave, 1984). It should be noted that the exact nature of this determination is moderated by level of self awareness as well as a sense of agency or self efficacy (Bandura, 1986; Betz & Hackett, 1987). Persons with high levels of self awareness and personal agency are in a better position to respond proactively to external circumstances and exert more control over long terms effects.

One of the major determining contexts is that of culture. The influence of culture is apparent when we consider a factor such as the role of significant others in decision making. In many cultures, making career decisions is not primarily an individual event, but rather an expression of the family group (Westwood & Ishiyama, 1991). From this perspective, a career decision can only be considered with reference to the collective needs and wishes of the group in which the individual is imbedded.

The influence of economic and political events can also be considerable and long lasting (Herr, Amundson & Borgen, 1990). Many of the people who lived through the depression in the 1930's have been influenced by the fear of scarcity throughout their lives. In our current economic and political context, cutbacks in education and a difficult labour market have helped to make young people and others more uncertain and anxious about their long term career future. For many this has led to a sense of helplessness and alienation, and has served to undermine effective career decision making (Borgen & Amundson, 1987).

The roles that we have assumed within our families and in the broader economic and social context also contribute to our career decision making perspective (Chusid & Cochran, 1989; Kenny, 1990). The expectations of others with respect to gender, birth order, health, and social status influence how we come to see ourselves and our interpersonal relationships (Ainsworth, 1989). These influences can be quite subtle and can serve to highlight certain traits and aptitudes, while undermining others. The impact of interpersonal roles have been well documented in the sociological and psychological literature. Some commonly noted examples include, eldest children assuming more responsibility (Dinkmeyer, Pew & Dinkmeyer, Jr., 1979), young women lowering their career aspirations (Phillips & Zimmerman, 1990), and disabled people becoming overly dependent (Schilling, Gilchrist & Schinke, 1984).

The factors that have been described thus far refer to events and interpersonal reactions which must be processed through the basic self structure. While general trends can be noted, there is always considerable individuality with respect to how people construe and internalize external events. This individuality is a reflection of personality, ability, and value differences (Covey, 1989). As mentioned above, people who have a high level of self efficacy and self awareness usually respond to challenges with considerable resilience and determination. Others, facing similar challenges seem to lack the necessary fortitude and persistence. Thus, individual difference must be taken into account when examining the foundations of career decision making.

Decision Triggers

The necessity of making career decisions depends on the activation of certain decision triggers. These events or people serve to highlight the necessity of making a decision and help to mobilize a person toward action. In some instances, these triggers are rather distinct such as graduation from an educational program, loss of a job, or pressure from a parent to leave home. In other situations the onset of the decision triggers seem to be more gradual. For example, a person may be somewhat dissatisfied in a job and may have some ambivalence about quitting and searching for another position. At some point, a certain threshold of dissatisfaction may be crossed and a job search may be implemented (Maccoby, 1988). The actual decision trigger may be something quite minor and be the "straw that breaks the camel's back."

The timing of decision triggers can vary considerably, even in situations that seem to be quite distinct. For example, students approaching graduation from an educational program all seem to have different times at which they come to grips with the impending career transition (Borgen, Amundson & Harder, 1988). Some may begin career exploration and job search months before the actual graduation ceremony. Others, avoid thinking about it until their schooling is completed. Some extend the time period for decision making by going on a holiday at the end of the educational program.

While many decision triggers involve something happening in the life of the person, other triggers are activated when certain events do not occur. For example, some people may have in mind that they will reach certain personal goals by a particular stage in their life. As they grow older and take stock of their accomplishments and life satisfaction, they may feel dissatisfied about their lack of progress and perhaps lack of meaning in life. These triggers often occur at age milestones such as "turning 30, 40 or 50."

Initial Framing of a Decision

As people move toward a career decision there is a need to conceptualize or "'frame'" the problem. The framing process is basically one in which people are taking aim in terms of a decision that they perceive needs to be taken at this point in time (Sloan, 1986). As they "'take aim," they bring to bear on all aspects of the problem the perspectives formed through the various determining contexts. Certain aspects of the problem are highlighted while others are diminished. The framing process includes both the problem definition and the preliminary strategies for compromise and action (Rogoff & Lave, 1984). To illustrate this process, consider the example of a person who has lost his/her job and construes the problem as finding a similar job in the same geographic area. The assumption contained within the problem definition is that there is a job "out there" that is close in proximity and that must be "found." While this may be an appropriate problem definition depending on the situation, it does leave out the possibility of creating a job for oneself, changing career fields, relocating, or returning for further education. In conducting a job search based on the above premises, the person would exclude any information which did not fit within the parameters that have been established.

Action

The initial frame forms the foundation upon which the first action steps are taken (Sarason, 1978). Information may be gathered and resumes submitted based upon the guidelines that have been established. It should be noted that action also implies inaction with respect to some possibilities. Certain steps will not be taken as a result of the focus that has been adopted. Using the example from above, the person will not look in newspapers outside of a particular geographic area. Any contacts that will be made will be done within the specified employment domain.

As information comes to light, certain external realities become evident and the frame that was initially set may need to be adjusted. The willingness to consider a change in frame often depends on some of the determining contexts that were mentioned above (Covey, 1989). Some people will be quite willing to alter perspectives while others will continue doggedly in their pursuit as originally framed. The challenge is to know when to put aside some of the original conceptions and consider other options (reframing). If people change too quickly, they may "sell themselves short" and end up with a position which is not in their best interests. On the other hand, people who rigidly adhere to their original frame may be out of touch with current market realities and may use up valuable resources and time in a futile pursuit. According to Meachan and Emont (1989) one of the greatest obstacles to effective problem solving is the failure to "break the mental set dictating that one ought to solve problems by oneself rather than asking a friend for help" (p. 20). Often consultation with others is essential for effective action and this may involve the process of reframing.

Reframing

The relationship between action and reframing is dynamic and reflects an ongoing process of decision making. According to Gelatt (1989) "decision making is the process of arranging and rearranging information into a choice or action" (p. 253). Carlsen (1988) highlights the transformational quality of this exchange in the following quotation:

> First there is conflict; then comes the search for new data; out of this comes the "aha" of the new insight; next there is a surging of energy as the individual, freeing self from the original conflict, moves to the final stage of a new integration of the old with the new. It is not a simple cumulative process but a transformational one. With increasing complexity of thought and self-knowledge comes increasing capacity to achieve personal creative solutions and new forms of knowing. (pp. 12, 13).

Within the reframing context, there is the review of information gleaned from action steps and the consideration of this information in light of the determining contexts that were described earlier. For example, a person may respond to initial job search frustration by thinking back to an earlier message that it is better to be working at something than not working at all. Coupled with this message is the emotional insecurity that is developed through job rejections (Borgen & Amundson, 1987). With this in mind, the boundaries of job search may be radically altered and the person may grasp at any job that comes along. Others, of course, have very different messages and will adjust their frames accordingly.

The activities within the reframing and action contexts are impacted and in turn impact the nature of the determining contexts. The person who has been successful over many years may frame career decisions and job search in a particular manner during the first few months of unemployment. Continued frustration, however, may serve to disorient and undermine the initial stance of agency and high self esteem. Anxiety and insecurity will flourish under these circumstances and the impact will be felt in both reframing and action strategies (Amundson & Borgen, 1987).

The nature of the determining contexts can also contribute to a state of indecisiveness. This is different from being undecided in that the person often fears commitment and puts themselves in a state of ongoing information gathering and reframing, perhaps with the hope that some perfect solution can be found (Sterling & Betz, 1990). Left to their own resources, people will continue to "spin," hopelessly and will avoid direct action. Indecision, however, does not mean that consequences will not follow. Not making a decision is a decision of its own accord.

Internal and External Influences on the Determining Contexts

As was mentioned above, reframing and action steps can contribute to changes within the determining contexts. These influences are felt both internally and externally in that new environmental information comes to light along with new perspectives on the self structure (Sloan, 1986). With career decision making, people become more aware of the current labour market and their personal reactions to career choice and job search. These additional insights can be positive or negative and also are not necessarily an accurate perception of the situation. For example, people can become overly pessimistic and unsure about their abilities. On the other hand, some can grow in strength and perseverance through the experience and can gain new insights into the labour market possibilities.

In addition to influences from the decision making process, there are also influences from other sources. Economic and political events are continually shifting, accidents occur, health problems arise and so on. These events affect determining contexts and in some instances can serve as new decision triggers.

Viewing the Interactive Career Decision Making Model from Different Vantage Points

In viewing the interactive career decision making model, it can be helpful to use different vantage points to highlight various aspects of the decision making process. Pepper (1942) has referred to these different vantage points as different world views and describes them in terms of a mechanical, organic or contextual perspective. While this differentiation helps to separate the three perspectives, it might be helpful to consider the ways in which the different vantage points are also complementary to one another. The work of the linguists Young, Becker, and Pike (1970) offer some interesting ideas in this regard. Young, Becker, and Pike (1970) suggest that experiences or events can be viewed as a particle, a wave, or a field. All three perspectives have validity and utility and can stand in their own right or be fused together to form a more holistic picture. Using this approach, it is important to be aware of the vantage point one is using and shift perspectives according to the demands of the situation.

A particle vantage point uses a "snap-shot" approach to examine what is happening at a particular point in time. In considering the decision making model from this perspective, the emphasis would be upon the current situation and what is deserving of immediate attention. For example, if a college student was trying to decide whether to major in Psychology or Economics, the focus would be on the relative merits of each subject area with reference to the student's current interests, abilities and long term goals.

The wave vantage point represents more of a dynamic process with increased emphasis upon the sequential and developmental nature of decision making. There is the recognition that even when a specific moment of decision making can be identified, there are usually many smaller decisions which undergird the decision as it is being made. In examining the college student's decision between Psychology and Economics, the focus would be upon how this particular decision evolved. What acted as the particular decision trigger, and how has the decision been framed and/or reframed and what actions have been taken thus far?

The third vantage point shifts attention to the field or the determining contextual issues. From this perspective the emphasis is upon relationships and patterns within the larger system and decisions are viewed in relationship to other people and situations. A field view of the college student's problems would focus on the determining contexts that surround the decision. What role do significant others play with respect to the decision being made and how do previous experiences with the educational system and labour market influence perceptions and the decision making process.

The advantage of using more than one vantage point has been recognized by a number of theorists, particularly with respect to the wave and field perspectives. Overton (1984), for example, has described this merger using the term contextual-organicism while Vondracek, Lerner, and Schulenberg (1986) have put forward the notion of developmental contextualism. Whatever the terminology, there is some utility in using more than one perspective in viewing career decision making as an interactional process.

Counselling Intervention and the Interactive Decision Making Model

Within the interactive decision making model there are two basic points of entry with respect to counselling intervention. The first method of counselling intervention focuses primarily on the development of the determining contexts. Counselling within this domain has a developmental or preventive focus. Rather than waiting for issues to arise, the counsellor works with the person to develop an increased awareness of how personal, social, cultural, and economic issues play a key role in problem conceptualization and decision making. In addition to increasing self awareness, challenges and new information may be put forward to encourage a reframing of certain dehabilitating internal messages. For example, a secondary student (with ability) may believe that he/she is incapable of pursuing further education after grade twelve. With encouragement and strength challenge from the counsellor, the student may raise his/her level of self esteem and be willing to consider a broader array of career options (Borgen & Amundson, 1992).

Moving beyond the preventive and developmental counselling efforts, there is also a need to address problems when they emerge through the career decision making process. The first step (**Relating**) in this intervention involves the establishment of a positive working alliance with the client (Gelso & Carter, 1985). This alliance is based on the interpersonal dimensions of respect, positive regard, and genuineness and agreement (agreed upon expectations) as to the nature of the counselling process. The working alliance forms the foundation of any help that is offered.

This first step in the counselling process focuses upon understanding the problem from the point of view of the person involved (Egan, 1986). Thus, it is essential to encourage the person to describe what has happened, their emotional and cognitive reactions, the action steps which have been applied, and their perspective on the future. The use of active listening skills is particularly appropriate during this preliminary phase. In terms of the model that has been described, the phenomenological description of the problem helps the counsellor to determine the nature of the initial framing, the decision triggers, and the relevant determining contexts. Depending on the timing of the intervention, the person may also describe the action steps that have been taken to this point in time and any reframing efforts that are underway. In many instances, the telling of the story in a sequential fashion to an interested person (counsellor) can of its own accord spur on new insights and serve as a means for reframing the problem.

The second and third steps (**Investigating** and **Synthesizing**) in counselling involve a focus upon the reframing/action dynamic. The counsellor at this point encourages the development of new insights by engaging the client at three different levels (1996). At the first level the client is encouraged to look back and review past accomplishments and transferable skills and attitudes. This review is necessary to reinforce the strengths that the client brings to the problem at hand. In reviewing the past, clients also need to be reassured (normalization) with respect to some of the emotional difficulties they have faced. The second level of reframing focuses on how clients are coping in the present situation. Excessive negative thinking is limited and there is an emphasis on affirmation from the counsellor and significant others to help strengthen resolve. Rational decision making strategies are explored and additional information gathering is stressed. The last level of reframing encourages a look to the future and new possibilities. New behaviors are encouraged and practised and success is assured by focusing on concrete and manageable action steps. The process of reframing is designed to change perspective and to offer clients a broader array of metaphors from which to examine their situation. According to Combs and Freedman (1990), "when people have only one metaphor for a situation, their creativity is limited. The more metaphors they have to choose from for a given situation, the more choice and flexibility they have in how to handle it. Finding multiple metaphors expands the realm of creativity." (p. 32). And, creativity is an essential ingredient in effective problem solving and action planning.

Taking action, the fourth and final counselling step (**Consolidating**), should be clearly in focus and flow directly from the position of reframing. The reality of most situations is that some form of compromise must be incorporated in order to proceed with action (Amundson, 1989). The action plan should include a sequential description of the steps to be taken, a clear indication of the involvement of others for ongoing guidance and emotional support, and a means for assessing the adequacy of the plan. The outcome of the action can often be felt at a number of different levels. The most immediate impact, of course, is upon the decision on hand. In some instances, however, the impact reverberates through the determining contexts and can in turn act as a trigger for new decisions. In these circumstances, the action serves as an important means for reconceptualizing some aspects of the self (Kegan, 1982).

Concluding Comments

The interactive decision making model that has been described incorporates a multi-disciplinary orientation. While there is an emphasis on individual perspective taking (framing and reframing) this is balanced with an awareness of the impact of political, economic and sociological factors on decision making.

In applying the interactive decision making model in counselling, it is important to keep in mind that decisions usually occur in clusters with respect to a particular issue. Thus, in analyzing decisions, it is helpful to be aware of what Stimac (1977) calls the decision passage. This passage can be conceptualized using a number of different metaphors. Daniluk (1989), for example, refers to a spiral model of counselling, Amundson (1989) to an hourglass, while Cochran (1990) describes cycles of change using the image of the life story. The interactive model of decision making must be understood and used within the broader framework of a decision passage. The ebb and flow of decision making usually involves changing contexts as well as the development of new perspectives. In coming to terms with this variability, the vantage points of particle, wave and field can be of considerable utility.

Study Guide Questions

1. Describe the process of decision making from an interactional perspective (i.e., determining contexts, triggers, framing, reframing, action, external influences).

2. How does self-awareness and personal agency influence the impact of determining contexts?

3. How can something not happening serve as a decision trigger?

4. What is meant by a particle, wave, and field perspective?

5. Using the interactive decision-making model, identify and explain the two points of entry with respect to counselling intervention?

2

Negotiating Identity During Unemployment

Norman E. Amundson

The way we see ourselves, our identity, is strongly influenced by how others see us. Social psychological theorists (Cooley, 1902, Mead, 1934, Sullivan, 1953, Goffman, 1959) have clearly illustrated the social nature of identity formation. According to Gilbert and Cooper. (1985) "our self conceptions hinge upon others' conceptions of us. In jointly constructing social reality, people mutually determine each other's identities - we become, in a sense, what others believe us to be" (p. 83). In coming to grips with this perspective, it is important to keep in focus the mutual interchange which influences the establishment of identity. This resembles in many respects a negotiation process whereby personal identity is established through ongoing interactions with others. McCall (1987) describes identity negotiation as a process whereby the individual strikes two bargains, one with the world and one with him/herself.

According to recent research, the actual content of other's opinions appears to be of less relevance to identity formation than how these opinions are perceived (Anderson, 1987). Our perspective and beliefs about a particular person or situation tend to heavily influence how we approach and evaluate the world around us. For example, a positive remark from a person can be viewed positively as a legitimate reflection of opinion or negatively as a strategy for manipulation depending on the context, past experiences and expectations. To fully appreciate and understand the identity negotiation process, it is important to keep in mind the perspective of the person.

In this paper I will be focusing on identity negotiation within the context of the unemployment experience. From my view, this perspective helps to explain some of the psychological dynamics that

This chapter is an adapted version of Amundson, N.E. (1994a) Negotiating identity during unemployment. *Journal of Employment Counseling*. 31, 98-104. Used by permission.

are observed and serves as a useful concept around which to base counselling interventions.

The Unemployment Experience

Studies by Borgen and Amundson (1987) of the dynamics of unemployment have clearly illustrated how an "emotional roller coaster" often follows from job loss. In this period of emotional turmoil, self confidence is lowered and there is a rapid drain of energy. The overall impact on identity is considerable.

The stories that unemployed people have provided regarding their unemployment experience confirm the considerable influence of others on identity. Within this context, the opinions of family members, friends, colleagues, employers, and employment counsellors contribute to a sense of well being or decline (Amundson & Borgen, 1987). The social pressures are often subtle, questions that are asked or not asked, bureaucratic structures that are put in place, and non-verbal actions.

In the midst of this swirl of interpersonal reaction to unemployment, it is difficult for most people to maintain a strong sense of identity, even in situations where there is a strong record of accomplishment over a number of years. Within a three to six month period most people seem to lose sight of many of their past successes and struggle with self doubt and life purpose. In many respects, the new self that emerges is only a shadow of the former, and according to some theorists (Chanowitz & Langer, 1985), represents a new entity which exists in response to the changed social context.

In terms of negotiating identity, it is obvious that for many people who are unemployed the end result of the negotiation is very negative. And yet at a point when everything seems hopeless, many people rise up and begin a process of renewal, a form of "re-negotiation." This resilience of human spirit is commendable and seems to reflect a strong inner drive for survival. The question becomes whether we can better understand this process of renewal and use this understanding to help people who are newly unemployed negotiate a stronger sense of personal identity. As a starting point it is helpful to take a closer look at the dynamics underlying successful negotiation.

The Negotiation of Identity

Identity negotiation is an ongoing process throughout life but becomes particularly significant during times of transition when boundaries are fluid. Successful negotiation of identity depends on putting into place a number of key strategies. The first step involves an understanding of personal interests, values, style and aptitudes (Amundson, 1989). For many people, reflection with respect to personal qualities and aptitudes is something which has received little attention. Defining oneself independent of job involvement can be an interesting and challenging task. Taking the time for self examination can help to establish a strong personal foundation for the many stresses which are often associated with unemployment.

In addition to self examination, it is also imperative to acquire knowledge with respect to the labour market. Rapid structural changes have created a very different climate in which to engage in job search (Krannich, 1991). Within this new context, it is important to recognize the necessity for up-to-date information, goal setting, flexibility, persistence, and networking. Positioning oneself and maneuvering within the current labour market may require a significant shift in perspective comparable in some respects to a paradigm shift (Amundson, Borgen, Westwood, Bailey, & Kovacs, 1992).

To facilitate the career exploration process and identity development, a program entitled "Career Pathways" has been developed (Amundson & Poehnell, 1996). This program is comprehensive and addresses both self and labour market career exploration.

The interplay between self and the labour market forms the nucleus of identity negotiation. As was stated earlier, contacts with employers, agencies and significant others, as filtered through the perceptions of the person, helps to define identity. It is difficult to control many aspects of these exchanges, particularly when jobs are scarce and employment services overburdened. There are some elements, however, which can be managed. Listed below are four factors which deserve special attention.

1. Support from Others

It is inevitable during a period of unemployment to expect some negative reactions from others. To counteract this influence, it is helpful to build a support network as a constant source of encouragement. There are many types of support network. Burton and Wedemeyer (1991) suggest that a person who is unemployed may benefit from viewing him/ herself as a corporate manager with respect to job search. One of the beginning tasks would be to set up a voluntary Board of Directors for advice and ongoing support. Another form of support is based on the self-help efforts of other unemployed people (Amundson & Borgen, 1988). This can be particularly effective because of shared experiences and the focus on helping one another through emotional, informational, and material support. Other forms of support can come through active involvement in community activities.

2. Managing Self Talk

Managing self talk (the private conversations we have with ourselves) during exchanges with others can be an effective negotiating strategy. It is important to keep in mind personal strengths and accomplishments and basic worthwhileness when coping with difficult people or situations. For a variety of reasons, many people may act and express themselves in ways that will serve to undermine self confidence. Within this context it is important to learn how to maintain a perspective that is positive and not susceptible to the negative influences of others. The other part of this picture involves the management of self talk which serves to distance and alienate others. Hiding problems or striking out may provide some short term comfort, but a long term strategy for health depends on open and genuine relationships.

3. Marketing

To be an effective negotiator, it is important to learn how to frame situations in ways that challenge negative assumptions (i.e., all unemployed people are lazy) and help others to see you in the best possible light (Borgen, 1993). Effective marketing depends on product knowledge (knowing oneself), packaging (planning and preparation), distribution (maneuvering within the current labour market), and selling (communication skills - listening and presentation skills). Marketing skills are useful in the workplace and are particularly helpful when coping with the challenges of unemployment.

4. Focused and Persistent Effort

Successful negotiation depends on effort which is both focused and persistent. Rather than using the shotgun approach to send out resumes, it is more beneficial to put effort into research and analysis to identify the most promising prospects. Armed with this information, a careful plan of action is derived which utilizes personal contacts. (information interviewing, networking), a well constructed resume, and ongoing involvement. With this approach fewer contacts are made, but the quality of contacts are enhanced through hard work and patience.

Applying Identity Negotiation Principles in Employment Counselling

For many employment counselling clients the need to re-negotiate identity is very real. As was mentioned earlier, the influence of others on identity formation likely is well underway by the time a person comes to see an employment counsellor, likely with negative consequences. Thus, the first step in employment counselling is usually an assessment of what has already occurred. Having the person tell his/her story is usually a good beginning. Contained within the story will be information with respect to the points that have been made above. Also helpful may be some additional questions concerning the nature of the self talk that accompanied each action.

An important element in this initial assessment is the determination of the person's perspective with respect to their current situation. To what extent have they lost confidence and what are they saying to themselves about their circumstances? How do they make sense (meaning) of their present situation and how do they view the future (Carlsen, 1988)?

Using the above information, the counsellor can begin to encourage, support, ask further questions, and challenge the ways in which identity has been redefined (assuming that some negative elements have been incorporated into the identity structure). Involving others in this social influence process can be achieved through involvement in a career reassessment group (Amundson, Borgen & Westwood, 1990). Some of the strategies that are particularly effective at this early stage include having the person review and specify skills and aptitudes illustrated by past accomplishments (with accompanying support and encouragement coming from others). It can also be helpful to normalize the situation (taking care not to patronize the person) by illustrating the reactions that are commonly associated with the stress of unemployment. These strategies and others are incorporated into the "Career Pathways" program mentioned earlier (Amundson & Poehnell, 1996). Challenging clients at this early stage should be carefully done and follow a strength challenge format (Borgen, Amundson & Westwood, 1993). With this approach, the emphasis is upon challenging people with their strengths rather than focusing on deficits. There also is an attempt to limit negative thinking.

As the re-negotiation process proceeds, it is important to keep in mind that the end goal is not simply a re-awakening to past accomplishments and strengths. With re-negotiation comes the opportunity to build on the foundation of the past. Renewed self exploration is encouraged along with a fresh look at the labour market. This new understanding must be linked with an awareness of the importance of support from others, positive self talk and marketing strategies in the negotiation process. Acquiring this perspective and the necessary communication skills requires hard work and practice.

Moving into action is the final step and, as was mentioned earlier, depends on focused and persistent effort. At this stage negotiation proceeds in a very different manner than previously. Careful planning and extensive preparation help ensure that contacts with employers are more positive. Support from others and renewed self awareness and confidence ensure that negative contacts are placed in their proper perspective. Using this structure the opportunity for win/win negotiation becomes more likely.

Undertaking this type of renegotiation process contributes to a more vigorous and effective job search but also changes in some respects the nature of the relationship between work and identity. Establishing self worth apart from the work role is an essential part of the renegotiation process. If a person uses their job as the main vehicle to create an identity, they will be in considerable difficulty when they find themselves facing unemployment. What is needed is a new foundation for identity which is based on personal capacities and attitudes rather than a traditional working relationship. This change in perspective provides inner strength and increases the capacity to cope with job loss and the stresses of job search; it also changes the nature of the working relationship.

The infusion of workers who have renegotiated their identity back into the labour force after a period of unemployment may have some long term consequences on the labour market. An interesting study by Patterson (1990) of unemployed managers and professionals indicated that reemployment brought with it some important side effects in terms of reduced employee commitment and loyalty. While the work ethic remained in place, there was a greater awareness of the importance of looking out for oneself while on the job. This included a greater awareness of the importance of the need to balance work responsibilities with family and personal concerns.

Concluding Comment

The primary advantage of viewing the unemployment experience in terms of identity negotiation is that the focus for both counsellor and client becomes one of process and change. There is always the possibility of renegotiation and the forward direction is one of seeking greater personal control within the negotiation process. As such, the concept of identity negotiation serves as a useful construct around which action plans and counselling interventions can be organized.

Study Guide Questions

1. How do others influence us in the formation of our identity?

2. When people are unemployed, they are particularly susceptible to negative reactions from people. At what period of time do most people find themselves riding an emotional roller coaster?

3. What are some strategies that people use to re-negotiate their identity?

4. What strategies can an employment counsellor use to assess how a client is viewing him/herself after a period of unemployment and promote a more positive identity?

5. How might the connection between identity and work role be changed through the re-negotiation process?

3

The Dynamics of Unemployment

William A. Borgen and Norman E. Amundson

Several researchers have studied various aspects of unemployment. Orwell (1975), Schumacher (1979), and Kelvin (1981), among others, have discussed the importance of work in defining a healthy identity. Perhaps the area of research that has received the most attention is that of psychological reactions to unemployment (Hill, 1977; Jahoda, 1982; Warr, Jackson, & Banks, 1982). Other authors have delineated some of the stresses associated with job search (Marsden, 1982) and have described factors that influence how people experience unemployment (Feather & Bond, 1983; Hepworth, 1980; Swinburne, 1981).

Although some of these studies preceded our investigation and others were concurrent with it, they all suggested to us that a comprehensive study into the nature of the unemployment experience was warranted. This view is supported by Heller (1976), Gurney and Taylor (1981), and Warr (1983). Thus, the purpose of our descriptive study of the experience of unemployment was to examine the evolution of psychological reactions over time and to determine some of the factors that moderate or intensify the psychological impact of the experience. The goal was to map out the territories or experiences related to unemployment that may help provide an explanation for the identity issues, psychological reactions, and job search stressors identified by other researchers. In this article we describe our initial theoretical model of the experience of unemployment and the interview-based research study we conducted to further elaborate the nature of the unemployment experience.

This chapter is an adapted version of Borgen. W.A., & Amundson. N.E. (1987). The dynamics of unemployment. *Journal of Counseling and Development*, 66, 180–184. Used by permission.

The Theoretical Model

Our initial model (Amundson & Borgen, 1982) of the experience of unemployment suggested that the feelings associated with unemployment are like an "emotional roller coaster" (see Figure 3.1). The suggested emotional cycle began with a reaction to job loss comparable to the stages of grieving suggested by Kubler-Ross (1969). When we examined all of the components of human needs (Maslow, 1968; Toffler, 1980) that a job could fulfill, it seemed evident that losing a job would represent a significant emotional loss. The stages of grieving in the Kubler-Ross model include denial, anger, bargaining, depression, and acceptance. She did not suggest that everyone would go through all of these stages in the same order or with the same level of intensity. She did suggest, however, that most people would experience facets of these stages. We have suggested that such experiences may also be true for people losing their jobs. This analogy is suggested by Finley and Lee (1981); and, although the comparison of the loss of a job to the loss of a loved one may seem a bit extreme, the analogy seems to have some validity to the extent that unemployment represents the loss of a significant life involvement.

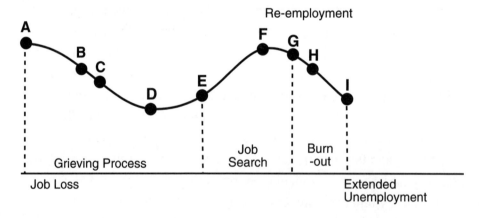

Job-Loss Grieving Process	Job Search/Burn-out
A. Denial	F. Enthusiasm
B. Anger	G. Stagnation
C. Bargaining	H. Frustration
D. Depression	I. Apathy
E. Acceptance	

Figure 3.1
The Experience of Unemployment

We suggested that, toward the end of this grieving cycle, people experience an acceptance phase highlighted by the recognition that the job is over and the job search must begin. We hypothesized that because looking for a job is a job, this phase would probably begin with a great deal of enthusiasm but soon run into trouble as people faced the realities of repeated rejections and unsuccessful interviews. The stress associated with this process seemed similar to the job burnout model suggested by Edelwich and Brodsky (1980). The burnout phase of the model included enthusiasm, stagnation, frustration, and apathy. We suggested that people might initially begin with some enthusiasm toward job search, believing that they had a chance at a new beginning and that they would be able to work in jobs that would be challenging and interesting. Given the current economic climate, however, we suggested that it would not take long for the harsh realities of job search to become evident. Under such conditions, people would probably stagnate in their job search activities and feel a sense of hopelessness and lack of progress. This stagnation, we suggested, would be accompanied by feelings of frustration and an increasing willingness to give up and do less in the job search area. The suggested end point of the burnout model was apathy, characterized by people having withdrawn from the job search and having decided that the whole situation is hopeless.

Interestingly, after the development of this model, we found a publication by Zawadski and Lazersfeld (1935) in which the typical course of the moods of the unemployed are described as a general feeling of injury, fear, distress, fury, numbness, calming down, hopelessness-fear, acquiescence, or apathy. Also, in a more recent article, Heppner and Downing (1982) described the job search and interview process for recent psychology graduates as an emotional roller coaster, with feelings ranging from excitement and elation to anger and depression.

Several other theoretical and research perspectives can be used in explaining the research findings cited and in lending credibility to the model suggested by Amundson and Borgen (1982). As a starting point, the importance of work in defining a healthy identity has been suggested by theorists ranging from Freud (1934) and Adler (1939) to Glasser (1965). Second, to the extent that people are out of work primarily because of forces beyond their control (i.e., a slow economy) and perceive themselves as being out of work through no fault of their own, they may react in much the same way as do victims of rape, incest, disease, and crime. Emotional reactions related to victimization suggested by the literature include shock, confusion, helplessness, anxiety, fear, and depression (Janoff-Bulman & Frieze, 1983). Third, when people find themselves in an extended period of unemployment that involves a sustained and unproductive job search, they may experience loss of personal power and feelings of helplessness may develop. The result may be a perception that their actions are irrelevant to subsequent outcomes, and they may begin to exhibit "learned helplessness" (Seligman, 1975). Peterson and Seligman (1983) indicated that when people face a negative situation, they invariably ask themselves "why?" Their answer plays an important part in determining their emotional reactions. If the person attributes the cause to external factors, the losses in self-esteem will be minimal. If, however, the person adopts an internal perspective and blames himself or herself for the negative circumstances, the result will be a loss in self-esteem.

Rapid shifts in labour market demands have resulted in a group of "new unemployed," those who formerly would have been long-term employees with marketable skills. If these are people who have been able to control what happens in their lives and who perceive themselves as responsible for their successes and failures, they may be vulnerable to what Seligman characterized as learned helplessness during an extended period of unemployment.

An Interview-based Research Study

Participants

This study was conducted in Greater Vancouver, a large metropolitan area on the western coast of Canada. Participants for the study were volunteers who were registered with Canada Employment Centres. Every effort was made to sample a broadly based group, and interviews were conducted by trained graduate research students over a 5-month period. The final pool of 56 participants included 26 men and 29 women. Of the participants, 21 (11 men, 10 women) were under 25 years of age and thus were classified as youth. The average previous yearly income for the participants was $16,050.

We decided to interview people who had been out of work for a minimum of 3 months so that there would be a sufficient period of unemployment upon which to comment at the time that data was gathered. The average time of unemployment for the participants was 9.2 months.

Procedure

The graduate research assistants conducting the interviews were not familiar with our dynamics of unemployment model (Amundson & Borgen, 1982). In training them to conduct interviews, we stressed the importance of letting participants tell their stories with a minimum of interruption or direction.

The interview procedure was designed to give participants the opportunity to talk freely about their experiences of unemployment and to focus on some of the high and low points. Using a phenomenological perspective (Fischer, 1979; Giorgi, 1975), we began the interviews with the following statement:

> *Please describe in as much detail as possible your experience of being unemployed. I would like you to include how you came to be out of work, what you thought about when it happened and your thoughts since, and feelings you have had during the time you have been out of work, and job search activities that you have tried.*

At the end of each interview (after about 45 minutes), participants were asked to focus on the critical incidents and to depict their experience graphically, on a time line that charted their emotions. These incidents and emotions, as depicted on the time line, were then discussed with each participant to ensure that there was a correspondence between the information provided in the interview and the summary graph. These discussions increased the likelihood that (a) the participants presented a valid representation of their experiences of unemployment and (b) the interviewer accurately understood the information that had been provided by the participant.

Data Analysis

We began our analysis by transcribing the interviews. We then had two graduate research assistants, who were involved in conducing the interviews but who were unfamiliar with our original model, summarize the data and divide it into "meaning units" (Colaizzi, 1978). Regular reliability checks (every 10th participant) were made to ensure that the same meaning units were being identified by each research assistant. The percentage of agreement in making these reliability checks was 96%. Using the summaries, the trained research assistants were then asked to transpose the information onto rating sheets. These rating sheets focused on several components: (a) stated shifts in emotion, (b) time sequence involved with the occurrence of particular emotions, (c) events or behaviors identified as accompanying specific emotional shifts, (d) coping strategies employed, (e) job search strategies employed, and (f) future expectations. Reliability checks were made by having every fifth rating sheet independently completed by the two research assistants. The percentage of agreement at this point was 88%.

Once the data had been coded, we considered the information in three groups: men, women, and young people. In each of these groups, the rating sheets and life line depiction of each participant's experience of unemployment were used to graphically represent his or her experience. More specifically, each time a participant stated a shift in emotion, the shift was noted and named, and an upward or downward pointing arrow was drawn to indicate the direction of the shift. For each shift, the relative spot on the figure was determined by the words used by the participant. For example, the shift feeling "somewhat hopeless" to "feeling cautiously optimistic" would appear lower in the figure than would "feeling hopeful" to "extremely enthusiastic." This process provided two dimensions: the horizontal, denoting time, and the vertical, denoting optimism or pessimism. The accuracy of the figure was checked by comparing it with the figure drawn by each participant at the end of his or her interview. In each case, the figure drawn by the research assistant was an accurate representation of what had been drawn by the participant.

Next, in each group (men, women, young people) descriptions were examined for similarities, and people in that group who had described similar responses to unemployment were placed together. Two research assistants independently sorted participants' descriptions according to similarity of experience. The percentage agreement on the sorting was 93%.

As a result of the sorting, a single pattern emerged for men and for young people, whereas two distinct patterns emerged for women. Further comparison indicated that one of the patterns for women was very similar to the pattern for men, and these patterns were grouped together.

The end result of the sorting process was that we derived three patterns of experience during unemployment. Pattern A consisted of 16 men and 13 women, Pattern B was composed of 6 women, and Pattern C contained 21 young people (10 men and 11 women). These patterns provided the basis for prototypical figures describing the evolution of emotional reactions to unemployment over time.

Results and Discussion

The research study began with a model suggesting that the experience of unemployment could be described as an emotional roller coaster. We suggested that the reactions to be expected initially in response to job loss could be closely aligned with the stages of a grieving process described by Kubler-Ross (1969). We also hypothesized that the stresses incurred in the job search would result in emotional reactions similar to those suggested by Edelwich and Brodsky (1980) in describing job burnout. The results of our study showed that the original model was generally representative of the experiences of approximately 52% of the people interviewed. The results also supported the findings of Gurney and Taylor (1981), Rump (1983), and Warr (1983), however, who argued that it is important to differentiate among groups when considering the experience of unemployment. Three distinct patterns, described below, were discernible in our study.

Pattern A: Men, Women I

This pattern was composed of 52% of the participants involved in the study; therefore, it is discussed in greater detail than the other groups. It contained all of the men over the age of 25 who participated in the study and women over 25 who were primary wage earners in their families. This group described shifts in emotion fairly closely aligned to the original roller coaster model, with some important differences (see Figure 3.2).

In the original model, the grieving period was graphically represented to be over a time period approximately equivalent to the job search phase. This did not prove to be the case for Pattern A. The grieving portion tended to be shorter than the job search period, sometimes being as brief as a few weeks and sometimes lasting a few months. People experienced some flashbacks to feelings of the grieving period during job search but usually did not dwell in this phase for long periods.

A variation in Pattern A occurred for 8 of the 29 participants (28%) in relation to their reactions to job loss. These people anticipated job loss and experienced a prolonged period of anxiety before actually losing their jobs. By the time they had left their jobs, they seemed to have gone

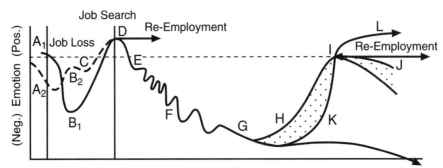

A₁. Initial negative reactions
    to job loss (shock, anger)

B₁. Reflection upon job loss
    (worry, anxiety)

A₂. Acceptance of job loss
    (anxiety, apprehension, denial)

B₂. Initial reaction to job loss (relief)

C. Acceptance of job loss
    (determined, in-control)

D. Acceptance of job loss (hopeful,
    optimistic, proud)

E. Initial reactions to stress
    associated with job search
    (pressure, discouragement, fear,
    anger, desperation)

F. Insulation from job-search-
    related stress (apathy)

G. Internalization of rejection
    (worthless, isolated, lonely,
    drifting)

H. Support/re-training (hopeful,
    understood, encouraged)

I. Maintenance of job search

J. Slippage to stress-related
    reactions

K. Re-assessment of self, values

L. Levelling (positive, changed)

Figure 3.2

The Experience of Unemployment: Pattern A

through grieving reactions and were ready to begin job search. They did not, however, immediately proceed with active job hunting. Instead, they were relieved with the termination of the job, and they took short vacations before beginning to search for new jobs. Once they had begun to search, however, their reactions closely paralleled the other participants in Pattern A.

We had suggested in the roller coaster model an initial enthusiasm phase, characterized by optimism that released energy for an effective job search. Our research findings indicate that this enthusiasm may have had some negative side effects. These side effects included the development of an unrealistic set of expectations about job prospects and, often, an overselling of self during job interviews. This overly optimistic attitude seems to set some people up for a heightened sense of failure in their later job search efforts if their expectations for employment are not fulfilled.

Another finding not anticipated in our model was a "yo-yo" effect, which occurred during the job search phase. Job rejections tended to make people feel worthless, isolated, and so forth. They would then rely on support from family and friends and start thinking positively to get ready for the next round of job search activities. This process resulted in the emotional yo-yo, experienced as erratic and rapid shifts in emotion that were often perceived to be out of the control of the person experiencing them. As job rejections continued, the low points of the yo-yo became lower and the high points less pronounced. This process tended to lead people into a period of decreased job search and increased feelings of worthlessness.

The original model ended with the suggestion that people would become increasingly discouraged in their job search efforts and would become apathetic. The research data suggests that many people did, in fact, become discouraged; and they experienced cycles of rekindled hope that became less pronounced over time, alternating with increased feelings of worthlessness. For the people in Group A, this period of reduced job search activity, characterized by feelings of hopelessness and despair, ushered in a phase of meaningful reevaluation of their worth as people and a new consideration of changes in their career paths. The increased acceptance of themselves was facilitated by a supportive environment, usually family, friends, or job search support groups. Along with this renewal of perceived self-worth, came the acceptance of the need to set long-range career goals and to begin activities, such as retraining, that could result in reaching these goals.

Pattern B: Women II

This group included 11% of the sample and was composed of women who were secondary wage earners in their families or who had sufficient financial resources to cope with a prolonged period of unemployment. Their expressed emotional reactions to job loss and job search were tied to a perceived loss of status and were described in less severe terms than those described in Pattern A (see Figure 3.3).

This group experienced a "time out" period, lasting up to a year, as they considered their options before looking for another job. As with the other groups, they began the job search with optimism; however, as time went on without success, negative emotions became more predominant. This slide downward was gradual, and the yo-yo effect described in Pattern A was replaced with a slow slide into feelings of worthlessness, boredom, and mild depression. This negative trend was reversed as they

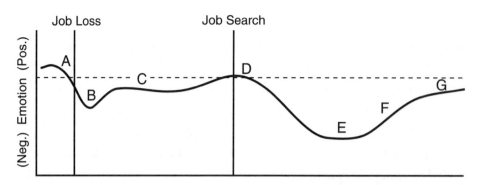

A. Anticipation of job loss
    (apprehension, denial,
    anxiety, illness)
B. Initial reaction to job loss
    (concern, bitter but fortunate
    angry, shocked)
C. Time out (rested, sick,
    leveled out)

D. Anticipation of job-search-
    (hopeful, positive)
E. Reaction to prolonged job
    search (bored, demoted to
    "housewife," self-esteem
    down)
F. Re-assessment of self, career
    options (hopeful, motivated,
    more confident)

Figure 3.3
The Experience of Unemployment: Pattern B

received support from others and began a period of reassessment of themselves and their career options. Considerable satisfaction seemed to be generated during this phase, and most believed that the unemployment experience had provided them with an opportunity for additional growth and development.

Pattern C: Young People

The people in this group constituted 37% of the sample and were mostly secondary school graduates who had little or no postsecondary education. They indicated that they expected to find employment easily and, when this did not happen, they were bewildered and frustrated (see Figure 3.4).

Because jobs did not seem to be readily available, they expressed little interest in continuing with the job search. They turned instead to other leisure activities, which helped to reduce their boredom but did little to further their chances of finding a job. Pressure from parents often become a problem for them, and they turned increasingly to their friends for support. They described many situations in which they were still in the role of "child" (e.g., being ordered to do things by parents, being unable to make decisions for themselves). They also described reactions to these situations that may have been expected of adolescents

14 or 15 years old rather than by young adults ranging in age from 18 to 24. That is, they complained about too much direction from parents and said that they felt helpless and unable to change their situations. This observation is consistent with the research findings of Tiggemann and Winefield (1984). Work plays an important part in the transition from adolescence to adulthood; and when young people cannot find employment, there is greater likelihood of a slowing down in psychosocial development (Gurney, 1980).

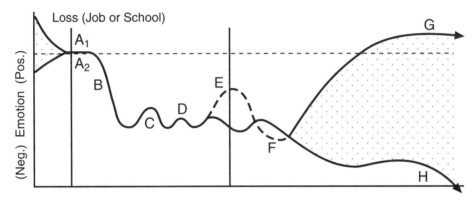

A₁. Reactions to loss (relief, enthusiasm)

A₂. Reactions to loss (shock, anger, fear)

B. Reflections on loss (frustration, anger, fear, boredom, lost)

C. Acceptance of loss (sadness, loneliness, boredom, anger)

D. Periodic Involvement (hopeful, useful)

E. Significant life event (personal or job-related; usually part-time job)

F. Continued unemployment (sadness, withdrawal)

G. Levelling involvement to substitute for work (worthwhile, loved)

H. Further negative feeling (fear of future, cheated, apathetic)

Figure 3.4
The Experience of Unemployment: Pattern C

Conclusion

It is evident from our study that, in many cases, unemployment leads to shifts in emotions and cognitions. This finding suggests that it is important to assess these reactions to unemployment to determine intervention options that may range from enhancing job search techniques to renewing self-confidence. Fineman (1983) noted that, without this type of awareness, many interventions may be a waste of time or even counterproductive.

This descriptive study represents an attempt to describe the unemployment process. Problems inherent in the design of the study include the use of volunteers and the reliance on participant recall. The first problem seems somewhat obviated by statements of those referring participants that members of the sample group seemed typical of their clients. A longitudinal or observational design would be required in addressing the second question.

Several possibilities exist for further quantitative and qualitative research investigations. Our research has provided support for describing unemployment as an emotional roller coaster. Additional research involving longitudinal studies would be helpful in charting the process of unemployment from this perspective. Also, other qualitative studies could further map out the process of unemployment for other population subgroups.

Study Guide Questions

1. In what ways can the grieving and burn-out process be comparable to job loss?

2. What similarities can be made between the psychological reactions to unemployment and the concepts of identity development, victimization, and "learned helplessness"?

3. Describe the three patterns of emotional reactions that are reported in this study.

4. In what ways do the patterns just described differ from the original roller coaster model?

5. How might the shifts in emotional reaction influence the employment counselling process?

4

Mattering: A Foundation for Employment Counselling and Training

Norman E. Amundson

A critical element for employment counsellors and their clients is the need to matter. Schlossberg, Lynch, and Chickering (1989) defined *mattering* as the "beliefs people have, whether right or wrong, that they matter to someone else, that they are the object of someone else's attention, and that others care about them and appreciate them." Mattering has been specifically studied in relation to juvenile delinquency and adult learning (Schlossberg & Warren, 1985). A logical extension is to consider the issue of mattering in relation to employment counselling training and service.

Schlossberg, Lassalle, and Golec (1988) have defined several dimensions regarding the perception of mattering. Four of these are described below:

1. Attention: The feeling that another person notices or is interested in you (e.g., when you enter a room people acknowledge your presence and make efforts to make you feel welcome).

2. Importance: Others seem to care about what you want, think, and do (e.g., people ask for your ideas and take the time to listen to you).

3. Dependence: You feel that you are a contributing member and others are counting on your participation (e.g., you are a member of a team and people count on your involvement for the development of ideas).

4. Ego-extension: You believe that others are interested in your successes and disappointments and actively follow your progress (e.g., others inquire about your well-being, even after you have moved to another task).

This chapter is an adapted version of Amundson, N.E. (1993). Mattering: A foundation for employment counseling and training. *Journal of Employment Counseling, 30*, 146–152. Used by permission.

Based on my research, training experience, and involvement with people who are unemployed, I believe that the various dimensions of mattering are critical to coping with the emotional challenges associated with work and service (Amundson & Borgen, 1987a, 1987b). Through involvement in mattering experiences, people meet their basic needs for relationships and meaning in life. Morale and self-confidence are boosted and this influences career selection, job search, and job satisfaction.

Mattering within Unemployment

For clients, loss of a job can be a truly "non-mattering" experience highlighted by feelings of despair, disillusionment, and anger. The first major shock can come when a person is told that he or she is no longer needed. The feeling of non-mattering continues as the job search begins and the rejections multiply. The accompanying emotional reactions have been described as an "emotional roller coaster" (Amundson & Borgen, 1982; Borgen & Amundson, 1987).

One aspect of the unemployment experience that is common for many unemployed persons is contact with an employment centre. Through unemployment insurance and employment counselling efforts, people interact with insurance workers and employment counsellors. These contacts are an important source of mattering and can help to offset some of the negative emotions generated through the unemployment process. If not handled properly, however, they can serve as another source of non-mattering and reinforce feelings of alienation and low self-esteem. The significance of mattering for Human Resources Development Canada (HRDC) is recognized within the following recent mission statement put forward by the Managers Task Group and the Project Advisory Committee (1990):

> ... we help people find jobs or collect unemployment insurance benefits between jobs. We manage the entry of immigrants, refugees, and visitors. We help workers and employers change as the workplace changes. We also help people learn new skills or start businesses. In short, we are is an organization where people matter (p. 11).

This mission statement highlights the fact that people matter at all levels and the challenge is to make this a reality.

Mattering Through Attention Giving

At the most basic level, unemployed clients need to feel that efforts have been made to make them feel welcome when they enter the office. The office should seem organized and efficient but also warm and inviting. Seating arrangements, line-ups, easily-accessed computers, reading material, and clear signs are important.

Contact with workers and counsellors must also reflect a focus on attention giving. At a practical level, this can be as simple as smiling and acknowledging those in the office. It can also be demonstrated by having support staff and counsellors walk to the waiting room to greet clients and escort them to offices.

Providing attention to clients is the foundation of an active employment counselling policy. This means not only attending to clients when they are in the office. but also taking an interest in their welfare during and after the unemployment insurance period. Often the only type of unsolicited attention that clients receive is based on the function of control. What is desirable is to make contact in terms of service delivery and follow-up whenever possible.

Mattering Through Acknowledging Importance

Unemployed clients need to be given the opportunity to express their ideas and needs and to be taken seriously. Our research with unemployed persons showed that support staff and counsellors often did not take the time to listen to what had happened to clients during their period of unemployment (Borgen & Amundson, 1987). The push for action can leave people feeling uninvolved and insignificant with action plans that reflect more about easily accessible services and programs than about personal needs.

One positive development that has taken place in Canada is the emphasis on individual or group service needs determination. Through this mechanism clients are informed about their rights and obligations and also about existing programs and services. They also have the opportunity to express their needs and interests regarding the various offerings.

The expression of importance should not be a one-time event. Clients need to feel significant through all phases of unemployment. Perspectives and emotional reactions shift in response to changing situations.

Mattering Through Helping Others (Interdependence)

Unemployment places people in a particularly vulnerable "one-down" position in relation to potential employers and to employment centres. There are often few opportunities for significance or for helping others. Some clients report that they feel worthless and feel that they are begging for a job and begging for the unemployment insurance benefits that are rightfully theirs.

Counteracting these negative feelings can be eased by placing people in a position where they are offering assistance to others as well as receiving help. The feeling that others are dependent on them for their ideas and services enhances self-esteem and reinforces a sense of mattering. The group context is particularly well suited to building interdependence. In a group there are opportunities for sharing experiences and ideas and for offering practical help.

Employment centres could also consider ways in which clients could participate more fully in the helping process. Perhaps a role could be found for unemployed persons to work as partners with employment centre personnel to extend services and assume more responsibility for their own care giving. These services could include everything from participating as consultants with respect to service delivery to helping organize a career library.

Mattering Through Ego Extension

In an organizational sense, ego extension refers to the sense of accomplishment that comes by helping clients to efficiently receive their unemployment insurance payments and to benefit from employment counselling services. To acquire this information, regular reviewing of client progress must be in place. This review must be driven by a desire for improved service. The information that is derived should be made available to counsellors and support staff at all levels within the organization.

At a more personal level, employment counsellors and support staff should be encouraged to follow-up the progress of their clients. These efforts should go beyond the concerns about control and focus on the positive gains that have been made and the need for any additional service or referral.

Personal and organizational efforts at ego extension are often avoided because of an underlying fear about what might be revealed or what might be required in terms of further assistance (or both). Solidifying a sense of mattering requires that this extra effort be made.

By engaging in meaningful follow-up, much needed information is gained regarding client needs and services.

Mattering within the Employment Counselling Office

Introducing mattering into client services requires that counselling personnel begin by examining their own sense of mattering. It is difficult to let others know that they count when you do not feel very positive about your own situation. Mattering starts at the top with the basic management philosophy and works its way through the various layers of a system. If clients are feeling that they do not matter, it is very likely that the support staff and counsellors serving them will have similar feelings. A starting point, then, for enhancing mattering is an organizational review of how mattering is implemented with support staff and counsellors. Do certain groups feel left out; are ideas flowing smoothly between managers and workers; and do support staff and counsellors feel that what they are doing is contributing to future development in the organization?

Building on this organizational and self-analysis, support staff and counsellors can begin to examine mattering with respect to clients in terms of the following three levels: (1) clients entering the system, (2) clients moving through the system, and (3) clients leaving the system because they find work or because their benefits have come to an end.

Mattering through attention giving seems to be particularly important at the first level. Mattering through acknowledging importance will overlap with levels 1 and 2. Mattering through giving help to others (dependence) is particularly significant in level 2. And mattering through ego extension applies at the third level.

The expression of mattering in these three levels should occur in an unconditional manner. In some respects this is similar to Carl Rogers's (1961) notion of unconditional positive regard. Clients should not be left with the feeling that their mattering depends on their fulfilling certain tasks or expressing certain attitudes. Although there will be many emotions, ideas, and actions that run counter to the wishes of support staff and counsellors, the fundamental notion of mattering for all clients must remain a constant.

Mattering has at its foundation a certain attitudinal disposition, and it is important to translate this into concrete behavioural indicators. Thus, it is not enough to merely suggest that we should be more positive toward clients. The specific ways in which the notion of mattering will be communicated need to be articulated. A very simple example would be to learn people's names and make a point of using their names in discussions with them. Leaving the office to greet people who are coming for appointments might be another strategy. There are countless ways, many with no budget implications, that mattering can be infused within an office system.

In attempting to express mattering counsellors also need to remember that the feeling of mattering is something that rests in the eyes of the beholder. Although a counsellor can take certain steps to communicate mattering, the perceptions of the client play a major role in interpreting the message that has been sent. This interpretation depends on many factors, including past experiences, expectations, physical health, and so on. Thus, in assessing whether mattering is happening, one needs to examine what is being communicated and how this is being construed in any given situation.

Mattering within an Employment Counselling Training Context

The training of employment counsellors must be embedded within a climate of mattering. The acquisition of employment counselling skills is enhanced when trainees feel that they are valued and a contributing part of the learning experience (Amundson, Borgen, & Westwood, 1990).

To achieve a mattering climate, trainers must begin by investing time and energy by carefully planning group activities and ensuring that physical facilities are satisfactory. Careful attention must also be directed toward the start of the training group and the initial stage of group development (Borgen, Pollard, Amundson, & Westwood, 1989). First impressions are important and set the stage for mattering.

The development of a mattering climate also is enhanced through recognition of the particular needs of adult learners (Schlossberg, Lynch, & Chickering, 1989). Trainees need to be validated for their past learning through education, work activities, and life experiences. They also may need to be affirmed regarding their ability to learn because of past negative experiences. Creating a safe and yet challenging learning environment helps trainees to experience fully a sense of mattering.

The feedback that is given during training should simplify learning and skill acquisition, but often is viewed by participants with considerable apprehension. To counteract this potential difficulty and promote mattering, a strength challenge feedback approach has been developed and used with considerable success (Borgen, Amundson, & Westwood, 1993). Many people are only too aware of their inadequacies but are unaware or are unwilling to acknowledge strengths. With the strength challenge feedback approach, strengths are highlighted through behavioural observation and people are encouraged to challenge themselves to expand and further develop their strengths for greater effectiveness.

Employment counsellor training has the potential to be an important catalyst for improved service delivery. To ensure impact on the job, however, requires involvement that goes beyond the training period. Trainees can benefit from regular contact that helps them make the application from on-course training to on-the-job service. Ego extension, as defined in this article, becomes formalized and an important part of the training experience. One illustration of this process is the competence maintenance project described by MacDonald (1993). Through competence maintenance the bridge between training and practice is solidified and there are opportunities for additional training in response to related issues that emerge in the office.

The concept of mattering has application at all levels of employment counsellor training. It is the foundation that gives form to the training experience. The success of training depends heavily on having participants feel that they are significant, that they are contributing members, and that they are of special interest to other members of the group, the trainers, and the organization.

A Concluding Comment

The need for mattering is critical during this time of rapid change and social and economic dislocation. The current turbulent times affect basic human needs such as meaning in life and the establishment of relationships (Toffler, 1980). Through mattering, interpersonal connections are restored, with positive implications for self-esteem and self-validation. In undertaking the challenge of communicating to clients that they matter, counsellors need to reflect on their own sense of mattering in the work place. In addition, employment counselling training needs to be based on a foundation of mattering to promote the learning and delivery process.

Study Guide Questions

1. Describe the four dimensions of mattering.

2. What basic needs are met through mattering experiences?

3. What practical strategies can employment counsellors use to provide a mattering climate for counselling?

4. How can the employment counsellor's personal sense of mattering influence the counselling process?

5. Describe how mattering can be applied to the training of employment counsellors.

5

Client Reluctance

M. Lynne Bezanson, Carol A. DeCoff, and Norman R. Stewart

Dyer and Vriend (1975) define reluctance as an "unwillingness, either explicit or implicit, that manifests itself in a desire not to co-operate in counselling. Either partially or totally, the prospective client does not really want to be a client."

Client reluctance as a legitimate problem facing counsellors has only recently received attention in counselling research and training. Most counselling theory has assumed that clients come to counselling openly and willingly, perceiving themselves as needing assistance, ready to work on their existing concerns and perceiving the counsellor as having appropriate assistance to give. Openness to a counselling relationship has often been taken as a given and reluctant client behaviour viewed as an indication of an ineffective counsellor. Counsellors faced with withdrawn, unco-operative or defiant clients have, as a result, had few resources to call upon for assistance and have tended to internalize these counselling experiences by seeing themselves as inadequate counsellors.

It is Dyer and Vriend's view that the majority of clients seeking counselling in all settings are reluctant in one way or another and that reluctance is a significant area for counsellor research and counsellor training. The importance of recognizing and resolving reluctance in order to facilitate effective counselling was supported in a research study done by Paradise and Wilder (1979). Using a group of university students, they examined the relationship between client reluctance and counselling outcomes. They measured client reluctance prior to receiving counselling and client satisfaction and perceived improvement following counselling. Their findings indicated that:

- the greater the degree of pre-counselling reluctance, the less improvement clients perceived in their problem areas and the less

This chapter is an adapted version from Bezanson, M.L., DeCoff, C.A., & Stewart, N.R. (1985). *Individual employment counselling: An action based approach.* Toronto, Guidance Center. Used by permission.

satisfaction they reported with both the counselling experience and
the individual counsellors, and

- the greater the degree of pre-counselling reluctance, the more likely
  that clients would terminate counselling prematurely.

There would appear to be an important link between client
reluctance and client goal attainment through counselling. It would
further appear that effective counsellors require an understanding of the
dynamics of reluctance as well as practical coping skills to assist them to
work through reluctance, when it appears, with clients.

The sources of reluctance are extremely diverse and the dynamics of
reluctance range from very simple to highly complex. While it is
generally true that all reluctance is born of fear, understanding of some
probable sources of these fears can assist counsellors to reach beyond
apparently negative behaviours in order to establish productive
counselling relationships.

Four common sources of reluctance described by Amundson and
Kenney (1979) are listed below:

Fear of the Unfamiliar

It is a truism to say that we fear what we do not understand and what we
do not know. This is the reality for many clients who have never
experienced a counselling relationship and do not know what they can
realistically expect from a counsellor or what expectations a counsellor
may have of them. They may be uncertain of what information to
divulge and what to protect and may therefore view the process with
considerable suspicion. Non-directive counselling can be particularly
threatening to clients who fear the unfamiliar and/or are misinformed.
Many clients are not accustomed to being listened to and having their
thoughts and feelings paraphrased and reflected. The purposes of these
interactions may be very unclear to them and the role of the counsellor
very hard to decipher. This of course may increase rather than decrease
their level of fear.

A degree of reluctance, suspicion or hesitancy in an unknown
situation is not necessarily negative. An unwillingness to trust a
stranger, albeit a counsellor, with one's personal concerns until that
individual has demonstrated his/her trustworthiness can also be
reasonable self-protection.

Refusal to Acknowledge the Problem and/or Take Responsibility for the Problem

For many clients, acknowledging to another that they require help to find a job, that their unemployment records are weak, that they have been laid off or fired, and/or that they simply do not know what to do can be demoralizing. Taking the position of "I don't want to be here"; "I'm only here because I have no choice" and "I'm sure you can't help me but what have I got to lose" can become a means whereby self-esteem is preserved. There is still a dominant social view that seeking assistance is a symbol of weakness and failure; and it is, therefore, frequently a challenge to seek assistance under the guise of not seeking it. Note that this type of reluctance is not to be equated with the very reasonable hesitation clients may feel concerning the competencies of the counsellor which are as yet an unknown quantity. The type of reluctance described here does not depend on the counsellor demonstrating that he/she is capable; it rests on the individual client acknowledging that an employment problem exists. He/she owns the problem. It is okay to be skeptical but it is also okay to seek assistance.

A further demonstration of this type of reluctance occurs frequently with clients who, while acknowledging the problem, deny ownership of the problem. The tendency is to "blame" the problem on external factors— "If it weren't for my boss"; "If it hadn't been for dropping out of school"; "If only they hadn't let me down." Blaming can become, for many persons, a system for avoiding responsibility. At the same time, such a system avoids making positive decisions to correct the situation. A frequently heard theme is "Even if I did that, it wouldn't make any difference—he/she/it would still be there." Cautionary notes must always be added when describing this form of reluctance. Individuals can have completely legitimate causes for blaming: firings are certainly not always fair; the employer is not always right; the unemployment level is unacceptably high; significant others can make life difficult for any individual. The reluctance problem emerges when a client gets "stuck" in the blaming stage and does not move into a more productive stage of "Given that is in the past, what can I do about my employment situation now?"

Job-loss/Job Search/Burnout

According to Amundson and Borgen (1982), emotions associated with job loss are denial, anger, bargaining, depression and acceptance; those associated with job search/burnout are enthusiasm, stagnation, frustration and apathy. Some of these emotional reactions can be expected to interfere with a client's openness to counselling as well as with his/her capacity to take or continue to take positive action to resolve an unemployment situation. Successful job search usually requires degrees of optimism, self-confidence, presenting oneself well and persistent effort. The realities of job loss/search/burnout create conditions for anxiety, loss of self-esteem, depression and apathy, all of which make the attitudes and actions needed for problem resolution much more difficult to attain. Clients who have experienced discouraging and disappointing job search will often react by retreating and withdrawing from the source of pain. The emotional need to avoid further rejection and failure may be more powerful than the motivation to continue active job search. These clients may appear to a counsellor to be unwilling to try, easily distracted and insincere in their reasons for seeking assistance. These behaviours can readily be construed as reluctant unco-operative behaviours. In reality there is much ambivalence in these behaviours—one side pulling for self-protection, resenting and distrusting assistance; the other side pushing for active resolution and wanting to believe that positive assistance will be forthcoming. Working through these protective resistances appropriately and gently is a counselling challenge.

Client versus the System

Employment centres often provide service to clients who have either been recently released from institutions or have dropped out of the educational system and whose experiences with "systems" have been negative or at least interpreted negatively. Some of these clients may perceive their problem to be the "system" and the "rules" of the system and expend much energy trying to "beat the system." The employment centre comes to represent just another bureaucratic system designed to work against them. Counsellors may receive the brunt of this form of reluctance because they represent the system and depend upon it for their livelihoods. Counsellors may not be perceived as resources of assistance but as dispensers of rules designed to make the client fit their system. To co-operate may mean, *ipso facto*, yielding to a system which is perceived as "out to get them." This form of reluctance can be difficult to deal with as it often manifests itself in a subtle struggle for power. The client wins if the counsellor fails in his/her efforts to assist. The client acquires a sense of power and personal control by defeating the system and proving that it doesn't work.

Secondary gains sometimes associated with systems can prompt a client's reluctance. The client does not want to be successfully helped because the secondary gain he/she is enjoying will terminate. This form of reluctance is common in the employment counselling setting where people receiving unemployment insurance benefits must register for employment. Every employment counsellor has experienced clients who would prefer to postpone the counsellor's efforts for the period of coverage so they can enjoy the financial benefits without interference. Counsellor's employment suggestions in these situations can be expected to be met with degrees of resistance and negativism. The secondary gain of unemployment insurance benefits is tangible and usually easily recognizable. Very often however, the secondary gain may be hidden and very personal to the client. Employment suggestions may be resisted because of fear that alimony or child support payments will be reduced if income increases. A client may have discovered creative ways to use time and may be reluctant to give up the flexibility and freedom which remaining on assistance may provide. These secondary gains place clients in legitimate conflictual situations which they may not feel comfortable disclosing. A counsellor, unaware of the dynamics operating, may be frustrated and confused by his/her apparent lack of counselling success.

A careful distinction must be made between clients who are reluctant because of secondary gains and clients whose employment skills are such that they will make less by working than they do by remaining on assistance. This latter situation presents hard, practical realities and difficult decisions which have to be carefully weighed and balanced and cannot be construed as reluctant behaviour.

Manifestations of Reluctance

The behavioural forms of reluctance are extremely varied, often subtle and frequently difficult to interpret. To some extent, manifestations may vary according to the source of reluctance. Clients who fear the unfamiliar may tend to demonstrate passive behaviours—silence, lack of open communication, evasion, hesitancy and nervousness. Alternately, depending upon the individual differences, they may tend to be extremely verbal, highly enthusiastic and apparently co-operative but avoid allowing the discussion to focus on their real concerns. Clients who are avoiding taking responsibility for problem resolution may demonstrate defiant and blaming behaviours, resent attempts to focus on their concerns, and place all responsibility for action on the counsellor.

Depressed clients because of job loss or burnout may appear lethargic, distracted, passive and negative. They may tend to jump to conclusions based on little evidence and appear overwhelmed by the difficulties and hazards which they may perceive inherent in any counselling action plan. Clients who perceive the system to be the problem and the counsellor as representing the system may appear unco-operative, distant, suspicious and notably non-disclosing or by contrast overly co-operative and artificially sincere.

In addition to reluctance covering such a broad range of behaviours, these behaviours are *not always* reluctant. Silence, for example, can be merely a demonstration of shyness and insecurity. Behaviours which may appear unco-operative on the surface may, with further understanding of the client, be a reasonable way of coping. The interpretation of behaviours as reluctant must therefore be treated carefully and tentatively.

Handling reluctance effectively is further complicated because it may surface at any point during counselling. Logically, one might expect reluctant behaviours to be present when initiating counselling, particularly during assessment; and that once dealt with, they would cease to interfere with counselling progress. However, clients may co-operate fully during assessment but resist when establishing precise goals to which they are asked to commit themselves. Contracting may produce resistance. Mid-way through a strategy when progressively more responsibility is being placed on clients, uncooperative behaviour may appear. Clients who are trying and not succeeding may become discouraged and withdraw from further effort. At the termination of counselling, clients may demonstrate unwillingness to discontinue the counselling relationship.

Counsellors need to be alert to reluctance throughout counselling and be open to working through these interfering behaviours. Counsellors need to be sensitive to the probable issues behind the behaviour—fear, anxiety, depression, insecurity, resentment for unfair treatment ,and resistance to being controlled. While there is no simple cookbook recipe for managing reluctance, there are conditions and techniques which can assist. These are:

- Managing your own reactions to reluctant behaviours.
- Creating counselling conditions of safety and clarity for clients.
- Creating counselling conditions which motivate clients.
- Specific counselling coping skills.

These elements are not pure and distinct and will overlap throughout the counselling process. For purposes of understanding, it is helpful to look at them as if they were distinct.

Managing Your Own Reactions to Reluctant Behaviours

Understanding that anxiety and suffering are often behind many reluctant behaviours is important to permit counsellors to call upon extra resources of patience and care. At the same time, these behaviours frequently activate emotional reactions which work against counsellor effectiveness.

Working with reluctant behaviours can be frustrating. Counselling time is limited and these behaviours impede progress towards counselling goals. Impatience, anxiety and anger are understandable counsellor reactions to frustrating counselling relationships. These very reactions, however, risk exacerbating and reinforcing client reluctance rather than resolving it. Counsellors who interpret reluctance as deliberate client behaviour may feel anger and irritation towards the client. These feelings are difficult to conceal and are likely to be communicated to clients as messages of non-acceptance and criticism. Many reluctant clients are particularly sensitive to messages of criticism. Criticism, for example, tends to increase depression; and depressed people are likely to respond by further passivity. Clients who are already resentful of the system and suspicious of the counsellor are likely to find that criticism reinforces their positions.

Counsellor anxiety is also a common reaction to reluctant behaviours. Counsellors are trained as facilitative helpers and it is easy to interpret problems in the counselling relationship as inadequacies with their own counselling skills and abilities. Counsellors may begin to feel awkward and insecure with a reluctant client. For some reluctant clients, this response fits their schema perfectly; for others who are in psychological pain, this response serves to increase their pain, self-blame and guilt.

Handling one's own emotional reactions to a counselling relationship problem is important to counselling effectiveness. Reluctant behaviours are the responsibility of the client; feelings of anger or anxiety with reluctant behaviours are the responsibility of the counsellor. Recognizing and owning these feelings without taking responsibility for the reluctance may seem obvious and simple. However, negative counsellor feelings such as anger and annoyance with clients are considered inappropriate in counselling. As a result, counsellors have a tendency to suppress such feelings and to pretend they do not exist. As noted earlier, these feelings do not disguise easily. Even if they are not readily perceived by reluctant clients, they will affect one's counselling manner and capacity to reach out to a client.

Through recognizing feelings and bringing them into personal awareness, counsellors place themselves in a position to be responsible for their portion of the relationship. Processing these feelings independently may avoid creating further inhibitions to counselling movement. Feelings of anger, anxiety, insecurity and irritation are important signals to counsellors to begin to look inward. It is helpful when doing so to have a framework for understanding anger and anxiety and to address specific introspective questions.

Anger usually occurs when the behaviour of another does not meet expectations or when the behaviour of another is considered unacceptable according to our own standards. The presence of unspoken "should" statements (i.e., "This client should be co-operative; I shouldn't have to put up with this; I shouldn't be wasting my time; This client should show more respect.") alerts the counsellor to the possibility that he/she is placing expectations on the client. Unmet expectations may be creating the irritation and anger. Often these expectations, upon examination, prove unreasonable.

Eisenberg and Delaney (1977) suggest that counsellors who recognize feelings of anger and irritation towards a client mentally process questions such as:

- Precisely what client behaviour(s) do I find disappointing or unacceptable?
- If I feel angry, I am making judgements about the acceptability of the client's behaviour. What standards or "should"s am I imposing? Are these reasonable?
- Is there fear behind my anger? If so, what am I afraid of? Is this reasonable?
- How do I understand the client's behaviour? What meaning does the behaviour have for him/her?
- What alternatives do I have?

Anxiety usually occurs when a person perceives him/herself as having a goal to achieve but feels blocked or unable to achieve it and further that the consequences of not achieving it will be negative and even harmful. Anxiety reflects a person's sense of inadequacy or adequacy in a presenting situation. Feeling awkward, uncomfortable or insecure alerts counsellors to examine how they are perceiving their own competence with a client. Unspoken messages are likely to revolve around— "I don't think I can help this client; This client is unreachable; I wish he'd ended up in Jim's office; I'm feeling put down and rejected; I don't know what to do next."

When feeling anxious and uncomfortable, Eisenberg and Delaney (1977) suggest that the following type of questions be addressed:

- What is it about this client or situation that I find threatening?
- Am I feeling competent about my ability to help this client?
- What am I afraid will happen?
- What is so bad about what might happen?
- What alternatives do I have?

The purpose for raising these questions is to check out the basis for one's own emotional reactions. Counsellors are doing for themselves what they frequently assist clients to do through counselling. This process may reveal to a counsellor that the anger or anxiety is something to be worked out alone and not to be attributed to a client. For example, a counsellor may find that the client is reminding him/ her of a previous client who was very difficult to help or that the specific behaviour is one which the counsellor has experienced negatively in another situation. Recognition of the sources for the feelings places the counsellor in a position to make adjustments to the client and to find alternatives which will not interfere with counselling effectiveness.

Having first checked one's own emotional reactions, a counsellor may conclude that his/her impatience, anxiety or anger are not unreasonable reactions. It would then be unfair to attempt to deny such feelings. The alternatives open to a counsellor at this point are to remain aware of the feelings but not disclose them or to present the feelings as information to the client. Particularly at the beginning of a counselling relationship, it is likely not constructive to the relationship or to the working through of the reluctance to present this information. Not enough is known about the client's world to assess if his/her behaviour is healthy coping, expected reactions to depression or deliberate behaviour. Later on, it may be necessary to confront the behaviour but not until the relationship is sufficiently solid to predict that such a confrontation is likely to benefit the client.

The first step in handling reluctance effectively is to handle yourself and your own reactions. Processing the feelings and understanding their sources permits a counsellor to avoid unwittingly reinforcing the reluctance. It also provides the objectivity needed to find alternative ways of remaining effective in the presence of reluctant behaviours.

Creating Counselling Conditions of Safety and Clarity

Establishing a collaborative relationship of mutual respect is core to assisting all clients. It is crucial in working through reluctance with clients. Many reluctant clients may require from a counsellor only the right invitation to enter into constructive counselling. The invitation, however, may require more time and patience from the counsellor than would be the case with non-reluctant clients.

Invitation is used here in a figurative sense. You invite a client to abandon reluctance initially through who and how you are as a counsellor. You have already processed your own reactions to reluctant behaviours and sought alternatives to avoid reinforcing the reluctance. Your effectiveness now is in your abilities to communicate caring, trust and honesty, to not judge a client's behaviour and to avoid coercing or manipulating a client into co-operating. If a client begins to experience you as competent, understanding and genuine, he/she is less likely to perceive a continuing benefit to self if the reluctance is consciously chosen. If the reluctance stems from fear or discouragement, a client is more likely to begin to perceive a connection and a source of encouraging support. Understanding that reluctance usually serves a protective function for the reluctant person and that it is not directed at the counsellor personally frees a counsellor from the tendency to be defensive. Once non-defensive, a counsellor can focus on relationship-building skills so that a client begins to feel safe and trusting. We discussed earlier that, to a degree, all reluctance is born of fear. Whatever the source for the fear, feeling psychologically safe is usually necessary in order for fears to reduce.

A second important condition involves counselling clarity and structure. For reluctant clients, clarity and structure reduce the unknown and begin to promote a feeling of being in charge of what will happen in counselling. One of the common sources of reluctance is fear of the unknown and yet it is surprising how frequently reducing the unknown is omitted in counselling practice. This is considered very important because:

- It assists clients to gain realistic expectations concerning what to expect from the counsellor and at the same time assists to dispel false notions and possible fears.
- It involves the client immediately in a decision which he/she must take concerning involvement in the counselling process. This provides the client with a sense of personal control from the beginning.
- Because information is not withheld or omitted, it promotes feelings of safety. These increase client readiness to become committed to counselling.

Initially, structuring includes sharing with clients the purpose, responsibilities, focus, and limits of the employment counselling process. They are reviewed here to reinforce what you have already learned and to draw particular attention to applications with reluctant clients. Recall that reluctance can appear throughout counselling and it may be necessary to review and clarify client understanding several times.

Purpose

In explaining the purpose of counselling, counsellors will want to stress that counselling is essentially a *learning* situation which focuses on assisting clients to make employment decisions, find and use employment information and learn employment related skills and behaviours if required. The kind of learning acquired through counselling can be used by the client in dealing with employment difficulties they may face in the future.

Responsibilities

The mutual sharing of responsibility for the success of counselling also needs to be explained. Clients need to understand that the counsellor's responsibility is to understand those concerns that act as barriers between the client and his/her successful employment, suggest courses of action, plan strategies with the client to assist him/her to attain the employment-related goal and assist the client to take the first steps towards achieving that goal. The counsellor may also stress that he/she hopes to create a relationship of trust and confidence so the client can discuss freely, explore without fear and practice new ways of approaching and resolving the concerns in a "safe" environment before trying them out in the work world.

The client's responsibilities also need to be stressed. These are to provide the counsellor with the information he/she needs to assist the client to work towards resolving the employment concern, to carry out the tasks agreed upon and with the counsellor's assistance to make the necessary decisions and to carry them out.

Focus and Limits

Two final areas are often helpful to clarify with clients and can be done simply and quickly.

Clients bring many concerns to employment counselling, some related directly to employment but frequently intertwined with a variety of personal concerns. It is, therefore, helpful to let the client know that the focus will be on the employment concerns and that, instead of attempting to work on all concerns at once, the focus will be on achieving one specific goal at a time.

In addition, the client may need reassurance that he/she can discuss concerns with you confidentially.

The responses of clients to open questions such as those listed below may provide the counsellor with important leads on the presence of reluctance:

- "How does this procedure strike you?"
- "How does this fit with your expectations?"
- "I've indicated how I understand what we will work towards. I'd be interested in knowing how you understand what I've explained and if it seems like a useful way to proceed."
- "As you can see, our working together will require effort from both of us. How do you see this for you?"

The time required for this clarification process will vary from client to client. For some clients, clarification during an assessment interview may be sufficient; for other clients, it may be necessary to clarify purpose and responsibilities several times. For clients whose reluctance is based primarily on fear of the unknown, the time spent clarifying is vital and may put the reluctance to rest. For clients whose reluctance stems from more complex issues such as depression or refusal to acknowledge the problem, frequent clarifying gives emphasis to the client's responsibility and control over his/her employment problem resolution. The operating principle is simple: the more counselling is demystified and the more clients feel they are in control of what will happen to them through counselling, the less reluctance is appropriate or necessary for their own self protection.

Counselling Coping Skills

The focus so far been on understanding sources of reluctance, dealing with counsellor reactions and creating, within counselling, those conditions of safety and clarity which work towards minimizing the need for clients to be reluctant. These do not deal with reluctance directly; rather they create an environment in which reluctance is more likely to be abandoned. With some clients, the environment is not sufficient and reluctance will continue to block counselling programs. It then becomes necessary to focus directly on the reluctant behaviour. How does one do this? The following four-step coping skill is suggested:

1. Acknowledge reluctance

In acknowledging the counsellor's perception of reluctance to the client, the counsellor may accomplish several things. Dyer and Vriend (1973) make the following points:

Acknowledging the reluctant behaviour communicates to the client that

(a) his/her feelings are acknowledged and understood, (b) counselling is not a process that pretends that feelings do not exist, (c) counselling does not avoid feelings, (d) the counsellor has an integrated personality and is strong enough to handle resistance in any form without being personally threatened, (e) by looking at the client and his/her behaviour openly and directly the counsellor is full of attention and respect for the importance of what is going on in him/her and his/her world, and (f) the counsellor is capable of avoiding moralization by showing the client that he/she is entitled to his/her behaviour, even when it is antisocial, ineffective, and does not have the impact it was generated to produce.

Acknowledging reluctance verbally is not simple. There is risk involved for both counsellor and client. The counsellor risks inflicting psychological pain, alienating the client, activating defences, and having to deal with defensive behaviour. The risk to the client is being faced with another's perception of his/her behaviour which he/she may not wish to acknowledge, accept, or work through. There is, at the same time, the risk that not acknowledging the reluctance will result in counselling being a wasteful investment for client and counsellor.

To acknowledge reluctance, the counselling skill of immediacy is useful. Immediacy requires that the counsellor (a) recognize that some unspoken feeling is in the way of counselling progress and (b) acknowledge this to the client being as specific as possible and staying in the here and now. For example:

- "I sense you are feeling uncertain about whether you want to continue."
- "I get the feeling that you are discouraged faced with so many steps to accomplish."
- "I notice that when we get to the point of discussing your responsibility in this contract, you seem to feel angered or irritated."
- "I'm beginning to feel uneasy. It seems that each time we try to focus on what you really want from counselling, you seem to want to change the subject."

Note that in using immediacy, one does not try to interpret the reasons for the client's reluctance. Reluctance, as we have seen, may stem from sources as simple as not knowing, to those as complex as repeated failure and negative self-perceptions. While it is important that you understand this, your concern is the reluctant behaviour insofar as it is interfering with counselling progress. Your concern is the here-and-now behaviour. It is, therefore, important that the client know that you recognize the reluctance, you accept the client being reluctant and that this is right now affecting the achievement of goals. While it is preferable for counselling progress that the client respond by clarifying what it is that he/she feels so it may be dealt with directly, reluctant clients may deny the counsellor's perception. If so, the counsellor accepts the denial and continues as the important message of letting the client know that you are aware of his/her reluctance has been communicated.

Notice that in using immediacy, the counsellor intervention is stated somewhat tentatively, leaving the client plenty of room to disagree. Notice also the importance of using "I" statements which state a counsellor perception or hypothesis and invite client reaction. "You" statements have a tendency to sound accusatory.

2. Involve the client in re-assessing the goal.

Several things can be accomplished at this point by re-assessing goals with the client:

- Where reluctance is a chosen way of behaving in counselling and the client does not want to continue this behaviour, reassessment offers a safe exit. The client, knowing that the counsellor recognizes and is ready to deal with the reluctance, may choose to begin to work seriously on a goal.
- Where reluctance stems from fear or depression, the caring of the counsellor in both recognizing client feeling and wanting to ensure that the goal is indeed what is wanted is communicated. Caring builds trust and invites the client to disclose what is blocking progress.
- The strong message is conveyed that while reluctance is recognized and accepted, the counsellor remains willing and committed to work with the client.

The counsellor might, for example, indicate to the client that a possible reason for not making progress and feeling uncomfortable may be that the goals established are not really those the client wants to or feels ready to work on. The counsellor and client would then proceed by re-examining each goal with the emphasis on involving the client in stating (a) how he/she feels about the goal, (b) how achievable it seems, and (c) how willing he/she is to assume responsibility for making an effort towards achievement of the goal.

3. Involve the client in looking at risk.

Earlier we discussed the fear of taking risks as being a potent factor in many forms of reluctant behaviour. A client statement such as, "That's what I want but I can't see myself achieving it" may mean for the client that the goals seem unrealistic for him/her or may mean that he/she is fearful to try in case it doesn't work. One of the interesting aspects of risk is that we often tend to think of the risks involved in doing something but seldom consider the risks involved in not doing something.

If reluctance continues, despite having acknowledged it and reassessed goals, it may be productive to assist the client to be introspective and look at both sides of risk. This involves assisting the client to explore dimensions such as:

- How satisfied/dissatisfied am I with my employment situation now?
- What are the risks to me if I work on achieving the goals?
- What are the risks to me if I don't work on achieving the goals?
- Is it realistic for me to hope to achieve the goals?

Obviously these questions are not asked directly in this form to the client and are explored in the context of an established relationship of respect. Many clients, particularly reluctant clients, can gain an important insight when they recognize that there is not only risk in changing—there is risk in not changing.

A variation of brainstorming is one useful method to assist clients to examine the risk in change. In conversing with you, the client may think of as many reasons for not changing as there are for changing, and change always involves the risk of the unknown. However, some reasons may be much more important than are others. This exercise helps sort out the consequences of changing and not changing and the comparative weights behind each consequence.

4. Use confrontation responsibly.

When you have passed through the previous three steps and the client remains reluctant to move forward into responsible problem resolution, it is necessary to responsibly and gently confront the client with the situation. A three stage model of confrontation follows (Peavy, 1980):

- Step one is a paraphrase of the client's perception (opinion, thought, etc.) to show that you accurately understand his/her position.
- Step two requires that the counsellor take the initiative away from the client by telling the client how he/she (the counsellor) perceives the client's opinions, behaviours, etc. to appear discrepant.
- In the third step, the counsellor gives the initiative back to the client who can accept or reject the confrontation. The open-ended question is designed to elicit a problem-solving attitude from the client.

All three steps are extremely important in achieving the goal of confrontation which is to facilitate the client's awareness of discrepancies in his/her behaviour. When a step is omitted, the result may be an unproductive client-counsellor confrontation.

In using confrontation, counsellors have to be prepared for defensive reactions. Clients may discount the information, justify themselves, or verbally attack the counsellor. Staying with the client without becoming defensive oneself becomes very important. Counsellors can support clients through confrontation by statements such as, "I know this isn't pleasant to discuss but I feel it is very important that we work it out together so that the counselling time we have will be worthwhile."

Appropriate confrontation may be very productive for clients. It may prompt clients to recognize their interfering behaviour and assume new responsibility and control, necessary conditions for problem resolution. It may also prompt a client's levelling with a counsellor and being open about the real issues, again necessary conditions for problem resolution.

To achieve these, confrontation must be done responsibly. Eisenberg and Delaney (1977, 102–103) outline the following conditions for responsible counsellor confrontation:

- Confront only if the relationship has gone beyond the initial stages of development or if basic trust has been clearly established.
- Do not confront another person if you do not intend to increase your involvement with him or her.
- Confront only if you experience feelings of caring.

Confrontation, as with any other counselling skill, is a helping skill. Using it must be based on a belief that the information in the confrontation will benefit the client. To achieve such benefit, the client must experience the counsellor as caring and respectful and perceive the counsellor as worthy of care and respect.

Reluctant Clients Who Try Hard —and Fail

A discouraging and disheartening moment occurs in counselling when a client has feared failure, has decided there is greater risk in not trying than in trying, has sincerely tried—and fails; that is, an employer isn't interested; his/her interview performance was poor; no training seat was available; his/her grades didn't meet the necessary standards, etc. The client has been reinforced in the old belief, "See what I mean; I knew I'd fail; I knew it wouldn't work out; there's no point trying." As a counsellor, what do you do now? You want to keep your client on the productive track of trying; you need to find a way to reinforce the client's effort and reduce the negative reinforcement he/she has just received; platitudes like "Rome wasn't built in a day" race through your head; but you know if you use one now, you may lose much of what has been accomplished. While not wishing to over dramatize. this is a sensitive and difficult issue for counsellors to deal with effectively. The following steps are suggested for your reflection and use:

1. Provide support and understanding.
2. Identify some success (however small) amidst the failure reported. Reinforce this.
3. Carefully assess all elements of the client's attempts to succeed and pinpoint the precise reasons that failure occurred. Failure may have had nothing to do with the client's effort but with a situation. If this is so, discuss and clarify it.
4. Accept freely your share of the blame for the failure's occurrence and make certain the client understands your willingness to acknowledge your fault. Be certain, however, that you don't accept more or less blame than is properly yours. It is possible for example that you thought the client was better prepared than he/she was; that the goal was too demanding; that you forgot to discuss a very important factor, etc.
5. Candidly and openly discuss the advantages of renewed, or new, action rather than dwelling upon what has happened.
6. Set a realistic, attainable goal if the previous goal was unrealistic in the light of the client's experience.
7. Adjust the strategy elements so that failure is not repeated. This may well include shorter report-in periods, smaller increments between steps, and an "early detection" system so that difficulty can be pinpointed before the client again experiences failure.
8. Better control over client experiences may be needed with safe simulations/modelling/practice preparing the client for the realities of the employment market.
9. The length of the intervention, that is, the length of the time the client works closely with you, may need to be lengthened, as well as the monitoring period.
10. Counsellor focus in all the above steps should be upon the possible and the positive evidence of client effort, motivation, and success already experienced.

When All Else Fails

We began by discussing that there are no magic recipes for working with reluctant clients. We have discussed counselling conditions which assist and a specific coping skill which may prove very useful with a large portion of reluctant clients. In all counselling settings, forms of reluctant behaviours which are very subtle and deceiving are encountered; and these are extremely difficult even for the most skilled practitioner to resolve. For some clients, the risks involved in giving up reluctance and moving toward change are simply too great and the rewards of remaining with the status quo too powerful to be abandoned. The responsibility of counsellors is to attempt to find the resources to motivate the client to assume increased responsibility and accomplish the desired counselling targets. Riordan, et al (1978) cites, among several counselling myths, two myths which are helpful to remember when all else fails:

- Every client can be helped, or its opposite, no unwilling client can be helped. Operating at either extreme is not only frustrating; it is false.
- I alone am responsible for what happens with this client. With reluctant clients, it is often essential to get assistance. In addition, the counsellor alone does not bear the responsibility for counselling outcomes. The counsellor has the responsibility to seek the resources. The client has the responsibility to change.

Study Guide Questions

1. Describe four common sources of reluctance.

2. In what ways can reluctance show itself through all the phases of counselling?

3. What are some ways that counsellors can deal with their own feelings when working with reluctant clients?

4. What counselling conditions set a climate that helps to minimize client reluctance?

5. Describe the four-step coping model that can be used to deal directly with reluctant behaviour?

PART TWO

Formulating an Overall Career Counselling Plan

6

The Centric Model for Individual Career Counselling

Norman E. Amundson

I n two earlier articles (Amundson, 1987, 1989a) I described the parameters of an individual career counselling model. I would now like to present a fuller description of this model taking into account feedback from counsellors and clients and the findings from a Competence Maintenance Project (Borgen & Amundson, 1992).

The career counselling model (see Figure 6.1) that is illustrated here includes four general phases of development with the expectation that there will be considerable back and forth movement between each of the phases. The length of time necessary to complete each of the phases will vary depending on the particular dynamics of the counselling relationship. The general expectation is that the second phase, career exploration and assessment, will require the greatest amount of time involvement. Despite the differences in time allotment, however, the importance of the other phases should not be underestimated. Without a good foundation or a good ending, the insights gained from exploration and assessment will be minimal. From my observations, most of the difficulties associated with counselling occur in the beginnings or endings (the bookends) of sessions.

Phase One: Relating (Readiness - Establishing the Working Alliance)

Creating a context of readiness, a working alliance between counsellor and client, is critical to the success of the counselling experience (Gelso & Carter, 1985). Establishing this alliance requires some attention to counselling fundamentals.

This chapter is an adapted version of Amundson, N.E. (1989). A model of individual career counseling. *Journal of Employment Counseling*, 26, 132-138; and Amundson, N.E. (1995d). The centric model for individual employment counselling. Unpublished manuscript. Vancouver: University of British Columbia. Used by permission.

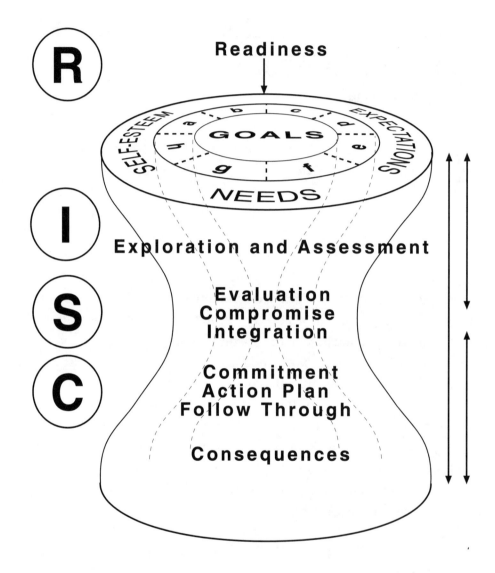

Figure 6.1
The Centric Model

Counsellors need to create a "mattering" climate where clients feel significant, valued and respected (Amundson, 1993). This type of relationship context is something that most counsellors would agree with in principle, but it can be difficult to put into place because of organizational hindrances, general unawareness, and personal issues.

The creation of mattering is something that starts when a client first enters the office. It is communicated through the general condition of the physical surroundings and by the way the office is organized. Sterile environments, lineups, confusing forms, and unsmiling faces all communicate a sense of insignificance and non-mattering.

The initial contact between client and counsellor is of particular importance in establishing a positive working climate. A simple act like going out of the office to greet a client and escorting him/her to the office communicates a sense of importance. Once in the office, arranging furniture to reduce physical barriers helps to establish a collaborative working environment.

Opening comments also help to set the stage for a closer relationship. The significance of this introductory period is often overlooked and viewed as nothing more than "small talk." Nothing could be further from the truth! It is a time when the world of the client and the world of the counsellor come together, a time of bridge building (Westwood & Amundson, 1994). In order to have a strong attachment there is a need for some basic connection. Perhaps it is as simple as a few comments about a sports event or a query about the design of some jewellery. In a cross cultural context it may involve a longer discussion about the country of origin, method of departure or relatives close at hand. Whatever the nature of the discussion, it is important to take the time to establish a personal connection.

Along with relationship building, there is a need in this initial phase to assess levels of readiness with respect to expectations, the fulfilment of basic needs, and self esteem. Some clients may not be ready to engage in the process of setting initial goals and for these individuals the counsellor must be prepared to make referrals, take action, or suspend the counselling process until a state of readiness has been achieved.

Most clients will be ready to engage in some initial goal setting and this requires the establishment of a common "wave length" between counsellor and client for communication. The four employability dimensions (exploration, skill training, job search, job maintenance) provide a useful framework for setting goals. Figure 6.2 illustrates the various employability dimensions and can be helpful in describing the goals, roadblocks, and the different pathways that may be chosen (Westwood, Amundson, & Borgen, 1994).

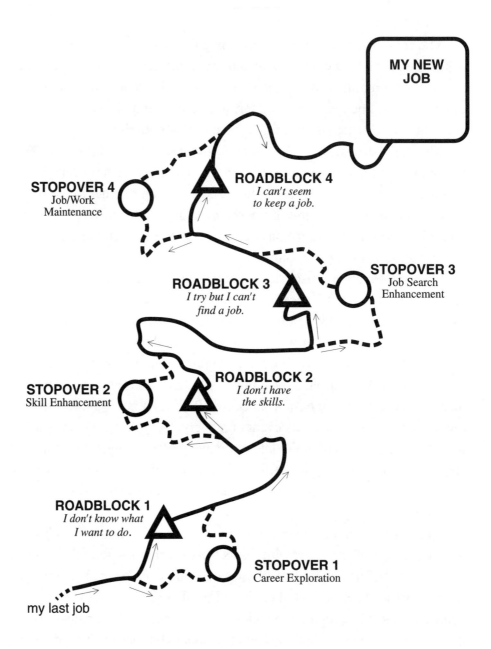

Figure 6.2
Employment Trip Planner

Establishing a common goal such as career exploration is only one step toward solidifying the working alliance. There still may be a need to clarify the nature of the career exploration process. Many clients believe that counsellors have a "magic" test that will take only a few minutes and will provide them with a clear career direction. Addressing this misconception early in the counselling process is essential. One of the tools that can be helpful in this regard is the "wheel" (see Figure 6.3) that forms the top layer of the counselling model (Amundson, 1989a).

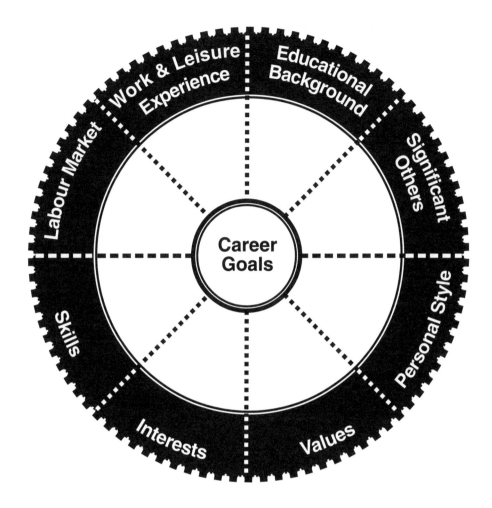

Figure 6.3
The Wheel

Using the figure of the wheel to discuss the various elements involved in career exploration helps to illustrate the complexity of the information that must be gathered. The wheel also can be used throughout the counselling process as a guide for exploring and organizing career information.

Phase Two: Investigating (Career Exploration and Assessment)

Career exploration and assessment occurs after the working alliance has been formed and it is clear that there is a readiness to pursue this particular employment dimension. The focus is usually on two different domains, the personal and the external. The wheel that has been mentioned earlier illustrates how both the internal and external come together to define more specifically the most promising career pathways.

A "Career Pathways" program (Amundson & Poehnell, 1996) has been developed to facilitate career exploration through both the internal and external domains.

Exploring the Personal Domain

At the personal level the factors to be considered include interests, values, strengths (skills) and limitations, and personal style. Each one of these factors can be explored and expanded upon. When choosing assessment measures it is important to be aware of what methods are best suited to client needs, level of counsellor competence, and the nature of the situation. Goldman (1992) comments that qualitative assessment measures are particularly useful for counsellors and provides the following reasons: "(a) Qualitative assessment usually is more informal and allows for more flexibility on the part of the counsellor in its use, as compared with standardized tests; (b) qualitative methods involve the client more actively in the search for self-awareness and can more readily lead directly and immediately into counselling interactions; and (c) qualitative methods, because they are usually not restricted to pre-set scales and scoring categories, tend to be more open-ended, divergent, and holistic in their interpretation and discussion" (p. 616). The primary disadvantage of qualitative assessment is that there is no comparative data. Thus, one is only left with self assessments or the opinions of others. While this may be an important source of information, there are times when a more objective assessment is warranted, particularly with respect to skill assessment (aptitudes). In some instances, standardized assessment can be particularly helpful.

When considering the various factors of personality, strengths (skills), values and interests it is possible to focus on each area independently or use a more comprehensive approach. If one is working separately on each factor a variety of assessment measures can be used. For example, with interests, measures such as the Self Directed Search (Holland, 1985) or the Canadian Occupational Interest Inventory (Booth, Begin, & Lavallee, 1980) may be helpful. With personality, the Individual Style Survey (Amundson, 1989b) or Myers-Briggs Type Indicator (Myers & McCaulley, 1985) are useful. Skills are often assessed using the GATB (U.S. Dept. of Labor, 1978) and values can be assessed using a variety of values clarification exercises.

While it can be helpful to separate each of the above factors for exploration and assessment purposes, there is also something to be gained by utilizing a more holistic approach. With this perspective the starting points are personal experiences which are analyzed in terms of patterns of action. These patterns reflect values, interests, abilities and limitations, and personality preferences. The personal experiences which form the basis for this exploration and assessment can come from either leisure/work accomplishments or from times of difficulty (Amundson, 1995c).

Exploring the External Domain

As the counsellor moves toward a consideration of external factors it is helpful to focus on the influence of significant others as well as review work and leisure experiences and the current level of educational (training) preparation. Often a resume will provide important background information with respect to education and work experiences, and the resume can be used as a starting point for acquiring more details during an interview. Information about significant others can be obtained by using a significant others questionnaire (Amundson, 1984) with general discussion.

Defining labour market options requires up-to-date information which can be obtained through careful research and information interviewing. Information needs to be acquired in two areas, the first being the identification of promising employment options and the second being methods of accessing employment and training options in a changing labour market (Amundson, Borgen, Westwood, Bailey, & Kovacs, 1992). The importance of maneuvering and positioning oneself for emerging opportunities needs to be repeatedly stressed and practised.

The Exploration and Assessment Counselling Process

What has been discussed thus far is the content of the counselling interview, of equal importance is the actual counselling process. Building upon the working alliance, counsellors are faced with the tasks of exploring and clarifying how clients perceive their situation. This understanding includes information about the various factors that have been mentioned above and an awareness of the problem solving strategies. The acquisition of this information occurs within counselling sessions, but it is also important to encourage clients to complete "homework" activities. This extra effort helps to make counselling more efficient and is a good indicator of commitment.

The counselling role is to collaborate with clients in a systematic exploration and assessment process. It is important to recognize that the very act of collecting information in this fashion can influence how the information is viewed. The discovery process usually begins with a careful description of information (story) but then often proceeds naturally to a reframing of the specific details.

The standard individual counselling model proposed by Egan (1982) describes the counselling process using a three-tiered model. The first step focuses on exploration and clarification, the second on developing new perspectives and setting goals, and the final step emphasizes action strategies. What is important to recognize with Egan's model is the fact that there is an ongoing interaction between problem exploration and the development of new perspectives (reframing). While these two phases are separated by Egan (they are not differentiated in the centric model), there is a recognition of the need for continuous back and forth movement. It is not uncommon to have new counselling problems emerge through career exploration; and when this occurs, there may be a need in some cases to return to a basic reconsideration of the goals set forward during the establishment of the working alliance. There is little to be gained by pushing ahead without a foundation of readiness and information.

Strategies for exploration and reframing involve movement from reviewing the past, to dealing with the present, and ultimately to looking ahead to the future (1996). Those strategies which involve a review of the past can be roughly organized in terms of normalization, acknowledging accomplishments, and transferable skills and attitudes. Those more oriented to the present include positive affirmation, externalizing the problem, limiting negative thinking, information giving, and decision making. In terms of the future, the emphasis is upon hypothetical solutions, modeling and rehearsal, new cycles of activity and focused goal statements.

A wide array of communication skills are essential to facilitating the exploration and assessment process. A counsellor must be prepared to engage in active listening as well as problem solving. Skills such as paraphrasing, clarifying, open-ended questioning, empathy (basic and advanced), supporting, limiting, immediacy, self disclosure, and confrontation (strength challenge in most instances) are invaluable.

In addition to skills, counsellors must also approach the task with sensitivity, curiosity, openness, genuineness, and respect for others. Understanding another person and offering alternate perspectives (reframing) requires a personal connection at the foundation. Without an infusion of these personal attributes, communication skills have little meaning.

Phase Three: Synthesizing (Evaluation, Compromise and Integration)

The exploration and assessment process described above will bring with it new insights and additional information. It is important that clients are not overwhelmed with the additional personal and labour market information that has been generated, but are helped to organize and evaluate the utility of the information in setting more specific career goals. Moving on to this next step does not mean an end to exploration, but it does recognize the need to move forward because of practical realities and because of the need for closure. In making this transition the issue of timing is critical. If the move is made too quickly, there will be resistance and lack of follow through. If the client and counsellor get lost in a never ending cycle of exploration, little will be achieved. The process of making the transition to this next phase can occur in several different ways. One rather novel approach is to have a five- or ten-minute break during the counselling session (Walter & Peller, 1992). The counsellor introduces the break with a statement such as the following: "We have covered a lot of territory today, and I wonder if at this point it would be worthwhile to step back and think about where we go from here. I would like a few minutes of quiet time to collect my thoughts and hope you will do the same. I am going to step outside my office for about 10 minutes to sketch out some ideas (a consultation with other colleagues may also be incorporated at this point). Here's some paper; please make a note of anything that crosses to your mind. I'll return shortly." The break helps both counsellor and client "shift gears" and move to a more focused frame of mind. Using a less dramatic approach, the counsellor can introduce other activities to help narrow the possibilities. One approach is to simply make a list of the potential advantages and disadvantages associated with a particular option. Another approach is to place the most promising option in the centre circle and then examine that option thoroughly from the perspective of each of the various factors around the wheel. The goal would be to reach consensus and look for patterns of agreement. A third approach would be to construct a grid and compare several options against a series of value considerations. As clients move into this next phase they often have to face the fact that some compromises may be necessary. This can be a stumbling block and a time when reframing is particularly helpful. There are many myths associated with the choice of career, three of the most common are listed below:

(a) The belief that once you make a career choice you are committed for life.
(b) The belief that the choice you make should be totally fulfilling.
(c) The belief that if you choose correctly you will be guaranteed a successful future.

To offset these myths, it is important to recognize the uncertainty associated with career choice (Gelatt, 1989) and the need to view career decision making as a process rather than an end in itself (Amundson, 1994a). The notion of stepping stones across a river or finding one's way up a steep cliff may be useful images to communicate that there may be different pathways that can be followed. At times it may be necessary to move sideways or even backwards depending on the situation and the level of personal readiness.

As clients consider compromises, it is important to separate misconceptions from core values and encourage a new integration which takes into account the person as well as market realities. It is essential to keep dreams alive and nurtured, even under difficult circumstances. The notion of short and long term planning can be a useful means to this end.

Phase Four: Consolidating (Commitment, Action Planning and Follow Through)

In order to move the career counselling process forward to the next phase, there is a need for consolidation—client commitment, focused action planning, and follow through. A context of client commitment is realized when the plan being followed is that of the client rather than that of the counsellor or significant other. Without this commitment there can be a lack of enthusiasm and motivation which leads to client resistance or reluctance and ultimately to a general breakdown of the planning process. Action planning requires the establishment of well defined goals. Walter & Peller (1992) describe the following criteria for the goal setting process.

(a) State the goal in a positive direction (i.e., what the client will be doing or saying rather focusing on the negative).

(b) State the goal in a process form (i.e., use action verbs—ending with
    -*ing*) rather than nouns).
(c) State the goal in the here and now (i.e., what will clients be saying or
    doing differently immediately after leaving the counselling session).
(d) Be as specific as possible (i.e., help the client to think through all
    the details).
(e) Focus on goals which are within the client's control (i.e., the actions
    that are anticipated should be started and maintained by the client).
(f) State the goal in the client's language (i.e., write down in the client's
    words what they say they want).

Using these criteria to state goals will increase the likelihood
of success.

Setting career goals can be a satisfying process as it provides some
closure and future direction. It is important, however, to ensure that
sufficient breadth in goal setting is realized. Given the changing nature
of the labour market and the possibility of unforeseen circumstances, it
is essential to build problem solving skills and to develop a series of
alternate plans. One way of expanding career plans is to ask "what if..."
questions to test the robustness of the plans that are being put forward.
Anticipating problems can only help to develop better plans and to
prepare clients for problems that might emerge.

Another important aspect of action planning is having clients put in
place the necessary emotional, informational and material supports. As
clients move forward, they will need a supportive context to help them
achieve the specific goals they are setting for themselves and at a
broader level to help them negotiate and maintain a new identity
(Amundson, 1994b). This supportive context must be broadly based and
be maintained on a regular basis to ensure its effectiveness. Specific
goals with respect to establishing and maintaining a supportive climate
should be established.

The successful completion of career goals depends not only on how
they are stated but also on client persistence and follow through. A
counsellor can help with this by checking with clients as to what has
been accomplished. This can mean having a follow up counselling
session or simply a conversation on the telephone. If there is a lack of
client follow through there may be a need to review the goals that have
been established and check client commitment.

Consequences and Further Action

As clients attempt to put into action their career goals there will be successes and failures. By following the above steps the chances for success will be enhanced, but there also may be occasions where additional exploration and re-assessment will be necessary. It is important that counsellors build this "reality of life" into their counselling and not treat those who require additional help as personal failures.

Also, as clients experience success and have new experiences they may want to engage in additional career counselling with respect to a new employment dimension. For example, they may know what they want and be able to find employment but have difficulty staying motivated on the job. Addressing new concerns will require further exploration and action planning.

Applying the Centric Model Within the Canadian Employment Counselling Structure

The four phases of the centric model are designed to reflect the processes within particular counselling sessions as well as providing a general framework for multiple counselling sessions. The Assessment Interview (ACEC) includes the phases of relating, investigating, synthesizing, and goal setting (consolidating) and as such represents all of the key counselling elements. When additional counselling sessions are warranted, the same four basic phases will be present. What changes is the amount of focus on any particular phase during each counselling session. One would expect that initially there would be more focus on relationship building, but the balance would shift toward the latter three phases as counselling progresses.

In many instances there is a need to go beyond the initial Assessment Interview and do some further exploration and goal setting. The current labour market is such that many people are having to consider major career shifts. Addressing this need requires a substantial investment of time and energy on the part of the client as well as the counsellor. The Career Pathways program (Amundson and Poehnell, 1996) is designed to facilitate this process, but ongoing contact with a counsellor is also advised.

There is no magic number with respect to how many counselling sessions beyond the Assessment Interview are advisable. Depending on the particular circumstances and the amount of homework completed between sessions, the number of additional counselling sessions generally ranges anywhere from three to six sessions.

Study Guide Questions

1. What types of situations might lead to back and forth movement between the phases of counselling?

2. Which counselling phase generally takes the most time?

3. In which phases do most of the difficulties associated with counselling occur?

4. Describe each of the four counselling phases.

5. What steps can a counsellor take to deal with clients who are not ready to proceed in counselling?

6. How can the four employability dimensions be used in counselling?

7. What are some of the advantages and disadvantages of using qualitative assessment measures?

8. How do the concepts of manoeuvering and positioning fit within a changing labour market?

9. What are some ways that counsellors can facilitate the transition from Investigating (Phase Two) to Synthesizing (Phase Three)?

10. Describe three common myths associated with career choice.

11. What are some criteria for establishing clear career goals?

12. How can counsellors help clients attain sufficient breadth in goal setting?

7

Action Planning Through the Phases of Counselling

Norman E. Amundson

Action planning is typically regarded as an activity that helps to draw counselling to a close, to consolidate learning, and to launch a client toward a new phase of self-initiated action (Cottone, 1992). Although this certainly is a valid view of action planning, it is limiting. In many respects, action planning can be viewed as an ongoing activity that is evident through all phases of counselling. The approach suggested here assumes that the client is an active agent in the counselling process. The client's entry into counselling is viewed as part of an initial action plan. Each step in the career counselling process carries with it implications for action planning. The focus of this article is on the articulation of these various facets of action planning and a discussion of their implications. The counselling model that is used as the basis for this exploration is a four-phase centric model that I have developed (Amundson, 1987, 1989).

Phase One: Relating (Readiness—Establishing the Working Alliance)

The very act of voluntarily approaching a counsellor is in some way a reflection of an action plan that a client is initiating. Clients approach counsellors with goals and some idea of how seeing a career counsellor is going to help them with their current problem. Counsellors also enter the exchange with conceptions of the nature of career counselling and the services that they can provide to the client. A primary function of the first phase of counselling is to create a climate of acceptance, in which there is an open discussion of perceptions and expectations. The successful establishment of this relationship helps create a working

This chapter is an adapted version of Amundson, N.E. (1995b). Action planning through the phases of counseling. *Journal of Employment Counseling*, 32, 147 - 153. Used by permission.

alliance and is critical to the success of the counselling experience (Gelso & Carter, 1985).

Many clients come to career counselling with misconceptions about what is actually involved. One common belief is that counsellors have access to a test that will tell the clients what career is best for them with a minimum of effort on their part. Another misconception is the idea that counsellors have knowledge about short training programs that will ensure well-paying jobs on successful completion. These beliefs and others are contrary to actual counselling practice and need to be openly discussed. Mutual understanding and agreement with respect to what can be expected from career counselling is a vital first step in developing a solid foundation for counselling.

As part of this initial phase, a foundation is laid for the interpersonal relationship between the client and the counsellor. As part of the client's action plan, there is the "checking out" of the interpersonal suitability of the counsellor. Clients are trying to determine whether the counsellor is someone who will treat them with respect, listen to their concerns, be flexible, be nonjudgmental, and be knowledgeable about career issues (Amundson, 1993). Counsellors, on the other hand, are also evaluating the interpersonal suitability of the client. They are trying to determine whether the client has a positive attitude, is open to suggestions, and is reasonably career mature.

Relationship building and the careful articulation and exploration of expectations can be enhanced through the efforts of the counsellor. Taking the time to find areas of common ground can play an important role in strengthening the counsellor-client bond (Amundson, Westwood, & Prefontaine, 1995). Discussing expectations and goals for the counselling sessions is also important at this point and helps set the stage for further counselling activity.

Phase Two: Investigating (Career Exploration and Assessment)

Following the clarification of goals and the establishment of a state of readiness, the client proceeds to a phase of exploration and assessment with respect to personal and external domains. In addition to in-session counselling discussion and activities, the client is expected to undertake various homework assignments. These assignments may involve contact with family and friends, personal reflection, research on the labour market, and so on.

The energy and enthusiasm expressed by the client in the counselling sessions and in the homework activities is an indication of agreement and commitment to the career counselling goals. In situations in which there is absenteeism, a lack of effort, and a failure to complete homework assignments, there is often a lack of mutually agreed upon counselling goals. The action plan of the client may be at variance with that of the counsellor, and this may account for the difficulties. If this is the situation, it is imperative that the counsellor return to the first counselling phase and re-examine the goals that were initially laid out.

Problems with client commitment during this phase may also be connected to the counselling strategies being used. As exploration and assessment proceed, the client may be faced with the task of reconsidering or reframing certain perceptions (Cade & O'Hanlon, 1993). Although this can be helpful, it also poses challenges and may have an impact on the goals that were originally established. For example, one client who was dissatisfied with her work in a secretarial position began career counselling with the goal of exploring other options. The information that emerged pointed out the many talents of the woman and challenged her to consider further educational training. The implications of this type of shift were considerable, however; and she had to step back for a short time to consider whether she wanted to continue the process. In her mind, the shift in options had gone further than what she had initially anticipated, that is, her action plan did not include this level of possibility. The end result was a new action plan and increased openness to more options.

A change of action plan during the course of career counselling can happen at many different levels. In some instances, a client may begin the career counselling process because it is a relatively "safe" forum in which to ask for help. If a bond of trust is established with the counsellor, other issues may be divulged. Under these circumstances the counsellor may be faced with changing the goals of counselling or making a referral. Whatever decision is made, it is important that the counsellor spend time reviewing the situation and developing a revised, mutually agreed upon action plan.

Phase Three: Synthesizing (Evaluation, Compromise and Integration)

At some point in the counselling process, there will be a time to pull together the information that has been generated and move toward decision making. The triggers for this shift may involve both a natural convergence of information and external pressures. Whatever the case, this change in focus requires a shift in action planning. Undertaking the initiative may require evaluation, some compromises, and ideally result in integration.

Selecting the appropriate time for this movement requires considerable skill and sensitivity. If it is done too quickly, the client may become resistant and there will be a lack of follow through. If, on the other hand, the exploration process is too extended, the client and counsellor may become trapped in an endless cycle of talk with little being achieved.

To facilitate a smooth transition, the counsellor can follow a number of steps. The starting point is often to let clients know in advance that the counsellor is considering movement to the next level. Summary statements and discussion of client readiness can be extremely helpful before initiating any change in direction. Once there is a general agreement with respect to the need for evaluation, the counsellor may want to introduce some decision-making exercises. These exercises focus attention on how information is consistent with various options and help to stimulate concrete action planning. Another novel possibility, suggested by Walter and Peller (1992), involves a consultation or "think" break during the session. This time-out period is designed for both client and counsellor and is used to think about possible actions based on the information that has been generated.

Because of market realities, during this phase the client may be faced with making some difficult decisions (Gelatt, 1989). Compromises may be required and when incorporating these in the decision-making process it may be helpful for the counsellor to help the client focus on both short- and long-term action planning.

Phase Four: Consolidating (Commitment, Action Planning and Follow Through)

Movement to this final phase requires the consolidation and establishment of well-defined goals. Walter and Peller (1992) provided the following advice when considering the development of appropriate goals:

1. Be positive when stating goals. Focus on what will be accomplished.
2. Describe goals in terms of action. Use action verbs (ending with -*ing*) rather than nouns.

3. Focus on the present. What will happen immediately after a client leaves the counselling session?
4. Be as specific as possible. Help a client to think through all the details.
5. Pay particular attention to those goals that are within the control of a client.
6. Use client language when stating the goal. This applies to metaphors as well as to specific statements.

Following these guidelines helps ensure that the client feels a sense of ownership and commitment to the goals that are put forth, and this contributes to a higher likelihood of success.

Although it can be satisfying to specify a particular goal or set of goals, some attention must be directed toward helping clients prepare for the unexpected and any barriers that might arise. Action planning within the current, rapidly changing economic situation is challenging. Any plans that are construed must contain within them a certain level of flexibility and robustness. One way of addressing this issue is for the counsellor and client to spend some time brainstorming and practising responses to difficult situations.

Another issue that must be addressed in this final phase is the personal readiness of the client to persist and carry out the plans that have been made. Achieving success usually requires self-confidence and support and encouragement from others. One of the major tasks of counselling is to help clients attain the necessary personal and social strength to follow through with their action plans. A "strength challenge" feedback approach can be particularly helpful in pursuing this objective (Borgen & Amundson, 1994). With a strength challenge approach, clients are encouraged to develop analytical skills and are validated by the counsellor in terms of the strengths that have been demonstrated. The goal of this approach is to have clients become more aware of their strengths and learn to apply them in a broader range of situations.

Ongoing contact and follow through with clients can also help ensure the successful completion of action plans. This additional contact does not have to be time consuming; it may simply be a short telephone call or a follow-up note. If problems do emerge, further counselling sessions may be necessary.

IMPLICATIONS FOR COUNSELLING PRACTICE AND EVALUATION

Viewing a client as an active agent through each step of the counselling process has implications for both counselling practice and evaluation. From this perspective it is clear that a counsellor must put considerable effort into establishing a collaborative relationship and understanding and working with the goals of the client. The active involvement of the client is essential at each step of the process.

Two common counselling problems can be minimized by approaching clients as active agents rather than as passive recipients. The first problem is one of overzealous rescuing in response to the issues expressed by the client. An excessive nurturing counselling stance may help reinforce client passivity and lead to a backlash in the form of passive resistance, that is failure to complete homework assignments, using "yes, but" to counter all suggestions. The end result of this type of transaction can be frustration, and ultimately a sense of victimization. Counsellor burnout can often be traced to a tendency to allow clients to take insufficient responsibility for their own behaviour.

A second counselling problem related to this issue is the failure to be sufficiently flexible when working with clients. Rather than acknowledging that clients can and will actively change their goals during the course of counselling, there is a type of tunnel vision that develops after clients have expressed their initial goal. In this scenario, counsellors view clients as active decision makers at the start of counselling but then assign them to a passive role once the goal has been set. In the more extreme situations, clients are given little opportunity even at the beginning to express their needs and expectations. Under these conditions the counsellor's agenda becomes paramount, and there is little attempt to match client and counsellor goals.

Evaluation of client progress is something that must start at the initial point of contact and continue through each phase of counselling. Some of the goals to be assessed are more process-oriented, whereas others focus more on the overall outcome. Danish, Petipas, and Hale (1993) have stated that process goals are more internally directed, whereas outcome goals must take into account the external influences. For example, learning interviewing skills (a process goal) depends primarily on client motivation and attitude. Getting a job (an outcome goal) is influenced by personal factors and the availability of jobs, especially in the current economic times.

Monitoring client changes must focus on more than final outcomes. Some of the additional factors that influence clients include goal redefinition, self-confidence, attributions, level of client activity, knowledge about support networks, knowledge about the labour market, and client satisfaction. A more comprehensive evaluation would be more reflective of the actual impact of counselling, particularly in a time of rapid change. This approach would be consistent with the point of view expressed in this article, namely, that clients are active agents who are involved in action planning throughout the counselling process.

Study Guide Questions

1. In what ways does the first contact between client and counsellor illustrate action planning?

2. What types of situations might suggest to a counsellor that there is a need to re-assess counselling goals?

3. What are some steps that a counsellor can take to ensure a smooth transition to the third counselling phase (synthesis)?

4. As a client attempts to consolidate goals in the final counselling phase, how should these goals be expressed?

5. What are some of the implications of viewing a client as an active agent during each of the counselling phases?

8

Refocusing on the Assessment Goal

M. Lynne Bezanson, Carol A. DeCoff, and Norman R. Stewart

Editors' note: *As was mentioned earlier, the centric model that has been presented is designed to cover the entire counselling process and the Assessment Interview as used by Human Resources Development Canada is one piece of this development. Within the Assessment Interview there is a focus on relationship, investigation, synthesis, and goal setting (consolidation)—the four phases of counselling development. This is not to say that the counselling process is complete, since in many cases there is a need to revisit the goal that was initially established. What follows is an important examination of the refocusing process.*

The last step within an Assessment Interview involves the delineation of the counselling goal. By now your experience in conducting Assessment Interviews will have helped you to realize that taking a client's concerns and translating them into goal statements is a challenging task indeed. You will also know that by moving with a client from constraints to contingencies to goal statement, considerable counselling progress has been made. Your client has now returned for further counselling services because he/she is unable to achieve the goal independently. *It now becomes important to review the goal and ensure that it is sufficiently precise to enable you and your client to evolve a definite strategy for successful goal achievement.*

This chapter is an adapted version from Bezanson, M.L., DeCoff, C.A., & Stewart, N.R. (1985). *Individual employment counselling: An action based approach.* Toronto, Guidance Center. Used by permission.

Review Assessment Goal

The importance of goal delineation and client commitment to the derived goal cannot be over emphasized. If upon completion of an Assessment Interview the following conditions exist:

- The assessment and intervention components of employment counselling will be handled by the same counsellor;
- The client remains committed to the derived goal; and
- The derived goal is precise and attainable,

the amount of time spent reviewing the goal will be very short and you will move quickly to planning action strategies. There is clearly no need to re-invent the wheel by repeating work that has already been done well.

What happens, however, when variations occur in the conditions listed earlier? When the assessment and intervention components of employment counselling are handled by a different counsellor or if time has elapsed between interviews, it is necessary to return to the goal stage to ensure that the client is still prepared to move ahead in this goal direction. Often goals can be like New Year's Resolutions. We feel totally committed to them on December 31, certain we will succeed on January 1; but by January 8, we may wonder why we made them, if indeed we remember them at all. Similarly, between interviews, clients may waver and be less certain.

Based on the Assessment Interview, you already have considerable knowledge and understanding of your client, his/her concerns and the intended goal. This information will be invaluable as you work to refocus.

The following sequence is suggested:

- Determine client understanding and/or acceptance of goal setting.
- Allow your client to dream.
- Check realism and/or adaptability of the dream.
- Ensure that goal is precise and achievable.

Let us look at each step of this sequence in detail.

Determine client understanding and/or acceptance of goal setting

The first thing you need to know is what occurred between sessions to cause the client to vacillate from his/her previous position. More understanding is needed. As a counsellor, you know that goals are needed for progress to be made but at the same time you know there are many reasons why a client may find goal-setting threatening.

Some possibilities which counsellors need to keep in mind are:

- The client does not understand why goals are so important to progress.
- The client has had the concern for so long that he/she cannot think beyond it to the more positive goal-oriented stage.
- The goal was, in some way, not really the client's, but represented more what the counsellor thought the goal should be.
- The client perceives some possibility of punishment if the goal is not attained.
- The work involved in changing is too threatening.
- The situation right now is not bad enough to justify the effort.
- The client wants someone to listen to his/her concerns but really is not motivated beyond having a listener.

Very frequently, discussion around the above points will reveal the source of difficulty and the client will move forward to re-establishing a desirable goal.

Allow your client to dream

When faced with a change to be made, there is a tendency to think small and stay close to the familiar, thereby reducing risk. The goal set during an assessment interview may have felt achievable in the supportive presence of a counsellor but on reflection may have seemed too risky. The tendency then is to scale down to something more conservative. The risk becomes that at a later time, the scaling down will be regretted and a client will wish he/she had been more ambitious in pursuing what was wanted but thought impossible or too frightening. This is particularly true in the area of unemployment where almost any job (even one in which a client has no interest) may reduce insecurity only to later cause dissatisfaction. It would obviously be a disservice to a client to encourage him/her to set sights upon an impossible goal; similarly it can be a disservice not to encourage a client to reach a little. With clients who have been caught up in the concern so long that they cannot see solutions, the technique of dreaming may be very beneficial and insightful. In all cases, as an employment counsellor, this technique may provide you with an important window into the client's world which gives you data on what your client would like to do or become.

Numerous leads can be used to let your client "dream a little" about the goal to be reached through employment counselling. Some suggestions follow:

"Let's take a few minutes, put aside all the hassles and focus on what you would like from our work together. If we could be successful at whatever we tried, what would you like to see changed as a result of our working together?"

"We've been discussing your wanting to decide whether a move west is a good idea at this time. Let's put that aside for a minute and try to imagine yourself working four years from today. What would you like to see? What would you like to be able to say?"

"When you think about all that is involved in returning to work after such a long absence, there are many, many factors to be looked at and we will certainly do that. Let's for now take a little distance from all those factors and look at what you want, regardless of whether or not it can be achieved. If I had a magic wand and could grant three wishes about your resuming to work, what would these wishes be?"

One of the interesting aspects of the dreaming technique is that it can provide necessary goal clarity. The concerns or complaints which a client initially introduces may immediately and correctly suggest an appropriate goal.

Many clients are not given the opportunity to dream a little out loud so they do it inside. This is of no help to the counsellor. Providing an opportunity to verbalize unspoken dreams during employment counselling can be most useful.

Wishful thinking is of course wishful thinking and it may be that none of these wishes can be completely realized in the short-term. However, as a counsellor, you are in a position to begin to use the information acquired to direct the counselling goal and subsequent action steps to take into consideration some of the client's inner world.

Check realism and/or adaptability of the dream
Following the process of dreaming used to help your client verbalize his/her wished-for goals, the test of realism is introduced. You must now consider with your client how to use the information from dreaming and

translate it into a counselling goal that is attainable. Counsellor and client must attempt together to establish a goal which meets at least some of the criteria of the wishes. One can readily see the increased chances for success when working towards a goal which is truly desired and at the same time within reach.

Ensure that the goal is precise and achievable

As noted earlier, after a productive Assessment Interview, the client's goal may be sufficiently precise and the client may still be fully prepared to work towards goal attainment. For example, a client may state something like the following: "I want to look at training opportunities which might be available. I've wasted enough time in dead-end jobs and I want to decide on a definite course to take in the next month." In this case, the goal is already sufficiently precise. In addition, the client is committed to working towards achieving the goal.

At this point in your reading, you may be thinking, "OK. I know I must end up with a precise goal but how precise is precise?" In deciding the degree of precision required, the following questions are key:

1. Does the assessment goal tell me enough that I can move immediately to a counselling intervention?
2. Can the goal be achieved within a reasonable time frame?

If you can respond "Yes" to both questions, then you and your client are ready to move on to the next step of the counselling process.

Study Guide Questions

1. What three conditions reduce the amount of time spent on refocusing the assessment goal?

2. If there has been a shift in goals, what steps can you take to explore this situation and derive a new counselling goal?

3. How can you tell that the goal you have set is sufficiently precise?

9

The Use of Metaphor and Drawings in Case Conceptualization

Norman E. Amundson

When describing an employment counselling case, it is common to use two levels of language. Hampden-Turner (1981) pointed out that there is the object level of language, which refers to basic physical description, and the meta-level of language, of which the metaphor is a good example. A metaphor can be defined as "a statement about one thing that resembles something else. It is the analogous relationship of one thing to another" (Haley, 1976, p. 65). The advantage of using a metaphor is that it allows the counsellor to assemble a complex array of information into a relatively simple visual image (Rule, 1983). This image not only describes "what is" but also provides a springboard for developing further insights (Hampden-Turner, 1981).

Case conceptualization bears some resemblance to the metaphoric process in that there is an emphasis on integrating an assortment of cognitive, behavioural, emotional, and interpersonal information into a synthesis (Loganbill & Stoltenberg, 1983). Metaphors can play an important part in arriving at this synthesis. Thus, in many instances, they are useful in furthering case conceptualization (Schon, 1983).

I would like to suggest a method of extending the usefulness of metaphors in case conceptualization by having counsellors make drawings of their metaphoric imagery and use these drawings in case discussions with supervisors and other counsellors. According to Amheim (1969), the principal virtue of the visual medium is that it allows the representation of objects in two- or three-dimensional space, as compared with the one-dimensional sequence of verbal language.

This chapter is an adapted version of Amundson, N.E. (1988). The use of metaphor and drawings in case conceptualization. *Journal of Counseling and Development*, 66, 391–393. Used by permission.

The Case Drawing Method

The method for using case drawings has evolved over a number of years in different contexts (e.g., case conferences, counsellor supervision, debriefing in a crisis centre). The basic approach is to encourage counsellors, as part of their case conceptualization, to draw a picture or make a collage that illustrates, metaphorically, how they see their client and his or her problems. In this drawing, they are asked to include how they see the case proceeding. The purpose of this task, which should be stated explicitly at the outset, is to help counsellors better conceptualize the case.

When presenting the drawing task, it is important to establish a set of procedures appropriate to the particular setting. For example, in some settings counsellors may take several days to think about their metaphor and construct a drawing or collage. If more immediate attention is warranted, a quick sketch of the metaphor may be all that can be accomplished. The advantage of the longer time period is that the counsellor can develop a more complete and carefully considered project In the shorter time period, the focus becomes the counsellor's immediate impressions after a counselling session.

It would be misleading to believe that responses to this drawing procedure are uniformly positive. Although most counsellors are excited by the possibilities, some are hesitant and others fearful There are many reasons for such negative reactions, including insecurity, lack of drawing ability, and inability to visualize. Thus, I suggest that counsellors be encouraged to try case drawings, but participation should be voluntary.

The procedure for someone making a presentation with a case drawing usually involves four basic steps. Initially, the case is summarized by the counsellor using the case drawing as a type of visual map. In the second step, the particular problem of the client (as it is represented) is discussed. For example, if a client is carrying a heavy load, a question might be raised as to whether this situation is of his or her own making or a result of external sources. In the third step, the focus of the discussion shifts from the client to the counsellor and the nature of the counselling relationship. Five key areas for exploration during this phase include:

(a) the sense of direction with respect to the counselling process;
(b) the level of optimism that the counsellor has when considering possible outcomes;
(c) the closeness and nature of the client-counsellor relationship;

(d) the extent to which the counsellor feels responsible for the problem; and

(e) the level of potency which the counsellor feels when assessing counselling interventions.

In the example of the client carrying a heavy load, it may be asked whether the counsellor is sharing the load, pointing the way, or helping the client unload some of the burden. Finally, the discussion shifts to how the drawing might be altered to reflect a different counselling orientation or approach. In some cases, the counsellor may choose to redo the drawing to reflect some of the insights that have been derived through the discussion. If a new drawing or a new addition to the existing drawing is made, it can serve as a specific reminder of new insight and, perhaps, a change in counselling direction.

Some counsellors have shared their drawings with clients and used this process as an opportunity to assess what has been accomplished and to set future goals. In this respect, the drawing becomes another counselling tool that helps counsellors and clients assess counselling programs and direction. Clients also may be invited to construct a similar drawing for themselves, and the two drawings can then be compared and discussed.

The overall impact of the case drawing method can be observed at several different levels. For some, the benefit seems to come from the development and drawing of the metaphor. As an illustration, consider the following statement made by one counsellor

As I started drawing, the impact of the meaning in the relationship between the would-be rescuer (counsellor) and the "rescuee" (client) really struck me and have me much food for thought. I enjoyed doing the drawing and completed it fairly rapidly, but felt disturbed by the dynamics evident in it.

For others, additional insight comes through the case discussion or the sharing of the drawing with a client. A more detailed case illustration is provided below to demonstrate the process and insights derived through the case discussion.

Case Illustration

A counsellor in a community college setting was working with a female client who was attending college full-time and undergoing considerable stress in her life. The client was 38 years of age, a single mother, on welfare, with 4-year-old twin daughters. Her ex-husband was behind on his alimony payments. Her boyfriend was an alcoholic. She had previously been accused by a neighbour of child abuse and had been asked by her social worker to enrol in parenting classes.

In trying to capture the various elements of this situation as part of a case conference, the counsellor constructed a drawing (See figure 9.1). In this drawing, the client is trying to climb toward a job and satisfying relationships but is dragging behind her an alcoholic boyfriend and her children. She is looking back at her children, the boyfriend, and other signs of problems (e.g., divorce, welfare, bad mother). Her financial aid worker, a teacher, and the counsellor are all standing above her as angels pointing the way toward parenting classes, retraining, assertiveness training, good mother, job, and satisfying relationships.

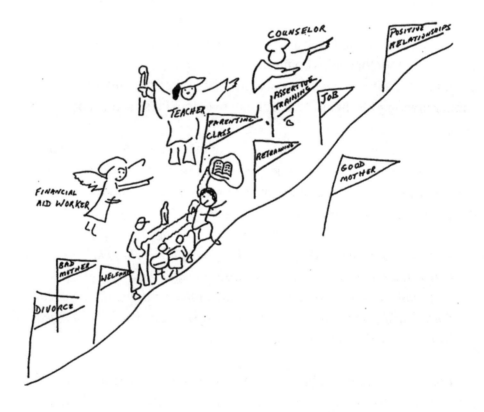

Figure 9.1
Case Conceptualization Example

In a supervision session, several points were raised with respect to this drawing that helped the counsellor increase her insight into the case in various ways. Some of the issues raised were

1. The angels might be pointing upward; but until they have the attention of the client, she is going to be looking and sliding down the hill. Getting the client's attention might involve coming out of the cloud and moving closer to basic realities.
2. The chains attached to the alcoholic boyfriend and the children are, in many respects, of the client's making. The client should be encouraged to consider how changes might be initiated (e.g., dealing assertively with her boyfriend, placing her children at her side rather than behind her).
3. The counsellor is placed furthest from the client, and the drawing of the counsellor's face is incomplete. If the counsellor is to make a significant impact, she will have to become more involved and supportive and move closer to the client.

Based on this feedback, the counsellor assumed a more supportive role and helped the client deal with these and other issues that arose through the counselling sessions. She constructed another drawing at the conclusion of the counsellor's involvement in this case. In this drawing the client was emerging from a maze of problems with her children at her side; the counsellor was no longer an angel but was now walking beside the client and facilitating the client's own decision making.

In summary, the use of case drawing provides a novel method of conceptualizing client problems and the counselling relationship and the means whereby conceptualizations are made concrete through drawings or collages. In some situations, this procedure can prove to be a useful addition for case conceptualization and group discussion. Research is necessary to determine under what conditions and with what types of people this approach is most effective.

Study Guide Questions

1. What are the advantages of using metaphors in case conceptualization?

2. What is the basic procedure in the case drawing method?

3. How do you handle situations where counsellors are reluctant to try case drawings?

4. Briefly describe the five key areas for analyzing case drawings.

5. How can case drawings done by counsellors be used in the actual counselling situation?

10

Perspectives for Assessing Career Development

Norman E. Amundson

This article illustrates how the perspectives of field orientation, time frame, and goal setting influence the assessment of career development.

The process of assessing career development is one that easily lends itself to different interpretations among clients, counsellors, administrators, and politicians. Misunderstandings are often a reflection of basic underlying differences in perspective. It is not the purpose here to articulate the reasons underlying these different points of view but rather to outline a structure for understanding how different perspectives are applied. The three facets of perspective taking that are examined include field orientation, time frame, and goal setting. With this information, implications for practice are be discussed and suggestions made regarding possibilities for a comprehensive assessment approach for career development.

Constructs Influencing Perspective Taking

Field Orientation

A number of images come to mind when considering the field orientation in which career development can be viewed. As a starting point, the reader is encouraged to imagine him or herself as a career development photographer capturing various aspects of a situation (the field) by attaching different lenses to a camera. In some instances, specific details may be highlighted by using a telephoto lens; on other occasions, a broader view may be attained by using a wide-angle lens. Each perspective has its own validity. One aspect of being an expert

This chapter is an adapted version of Amundson, N.E. (1994b). Perspectives for assessing career development. *Journal of Employment Counseling.* 31, 147-154. Used by permission.

photographer is learning how to use different lenses to accomplish particular goals. Problems occur if you are unable or unaware of how to use different lenses. Also, in communicating and appreciating the work of others, it helps to have experience with different lenses.

In developing an assessment approach for career development, it is important to be aware of what level of detail is needed (the type of lens that needs to be used). In some situations, an in-depth analysis may be warranted; whereas in others, an indication of general trends may be more useful. Also, there may be differences in focus if you broaden the context for a particular client to include not just the individual but also significant others. Forrest (1994), for example, suggests that given our current social trends, it may be more appropriate in many situations to consider couples as the basic unit for conducting career counselling. The case could also be made for including a broader range of family and other primary group members depending on the nature of the situation (Amundson, 1989). Including primary group members has major implications for how career assessment is conducted. As a starting point, information needs to be gathered using procedures such as a significant others questionnaire or a joint interview (Amundson, 1984).

Field orientation also plays a major part in determining the interpersonal nature of the assessment process. As one moves closer to a situation (telephoto lens), the natural inclination is to assume a more involved and active role. Significant differences between involved (active) and uninvolved (passive) perceivers with respect to attributions, evaluation bias, and cognitive processing have been described in the research literature (Manusov, 1993). Assessment bias, as described by Haverkamp (1994), reflects the different levels of field orientation that can be assumed when undertaking career assessment.

Time Frame

The image of the photographer that has been used provides a fixed view of career development, a snapshot approach to perspective taking. This view emphasizes different elements of the field (i.e., greater breadth and different levels of detail and involvement), but does not fully take into account past events or future planning. Young, Becker, and Pike (1970) used the image of a particle and a wave to make this distinction. The particle exists as a separate entity in time and space; whereas the wave has a history and a future direction. Thus, to extend the notion of perspective taking, it may be helpful to add the dimension of movement through time. Career development can be viewed as wave-like patterns moving through time and space. The current tumultuous labour market suggests that the pathways over or through which the waves would pass would often be unstable and difficult to assess (Krannich, 1991). Capturing the wave perspective may require an examination of past performance and of future expectations. Assessment over an extended period of time seems to be particularly well suited to people who are facing structural employment issues. People who are having to reassess their career direction, obtain additional training, or involve themselves in the labour market in new ways (i.e., as consultants, contingency workers, or self-employed) require an assessment approach that has a longer time base. Problem solving and goal attainment within this context need to be viewed from a sequential and interactive perspective (Amundson, 1994). Viewing career development using a time-based sequence is certainly consistent with the very notion of development. Movement or growth is ongoing throughout life and is captured in the stories or narratives that are used in describing life experiences (Cochran, 1990; Young & Collin, 1992). Life stories help make career development a reality and bring together movement through past, present, and future.

Goal Setting

The bottom line for many people respecting to career development is what particular goals are pursued and to what extent the goals are realized. At one level this seems to be a fairly straightforward question, but there are different values and perspectives with respect to the types of goals that are put forward.

Some goals are more process oriented; whereas others emphasize outcomes. Process goals might involve gains in insight, motivation, or activity. Outcome goals, however, concern themselves primarily with achievements such as getting a job or getting admitted to a training or educational program. A key distinguishing feature between outcome and process goals seems to be the level of personal control (Danish, Petipas, & Hale, 1993). Process goals are mostly realized through internal factors; whereas outcome goals are more externally influenced. For example, acquiring and applying job-search skills allow people to position themselves for job openings. The actual acquisition of the job, however, depends heavily on economic and political factors that determine job availability. The relationship between process goals and outcome goals needs to be clearly articulated as part of career development assessment. This exploration and clarification can help clients focus more on the areas where it is most productive for them to direct their efforts. It also can help clients to recognize the limits of personal responsibility. The following is a list of some key process goals that have been identified by Amundson (1989); Amundson, Borgen, and Tench (in press); and Herr (1993):

1. **Knowledge of self**: a clear understanding of abilities, values, interests, and personal style
2. **Knowledge of the social and labour market system**: an understanding of current social and labour market trends, emerging possibilities, and unwritten rules
3. **Personal flexibility**: the willingness to take risks, to think creatively, to move away from traditional comfort zones, and to approach learning as a lifelong activity
4. **Relationships with others**: The ability to interact positively with peers and with those in authority and to form appropriate support networks
5. **Skills**: Relevant behavioural and cognitive skills with respect to career decision making, educational planning, job search, and job maintenance
6. **Attitudes**: optimism, self-confidence, self-efficacy, and a willingness to persist (hardiness) in the face of ongoing challenges

Taken together, the six process goals just mentioned contribute to a state of readiness and involvement regarding the pursuit of outcome goals such as education and training or work. They also are consistent with other goals such as self-employment (an integrated process-outcome goal) and involvement in leisure pursuits.

The relationship between process and outcome goals has begun to be questioned in countries such as Denmark (Plant, 1993). What has been proposed is that client "activation" be regarded as a sufficient goal in itself. With this perspective, the focus is on encouraging an active and meaningful life irrespective of involvement in paid work. This suggestion points in an interesting direction and suggests that process goals should be considered as important milestones in their own right.

Illustrations of the Impact of Different Perspectives on Assessment

Using the information and images that have been introduced in the previous section, it is clear that career development assessment can be approached from a number of perspectives. To illustrate in practical terms how the approach used can influence assessment, consider the following situations.

Situation 1 - Field Orientation

Samuel was unemployed and unable to find a suitable job using his skills in English literature. He approached an employment counsellor and indicated that he wanted a thorough assessment so that he could get a clear sense of career direction. He stated that his wife, a receptionist in a doctor's office, had supported him through his graduate program and he wanted to make sure that he now pursued a career direction that would make maximum use of his talents.

In responding to this request, the counsellor initiated a comprehensive testing program using quantitative and qualitative measures. This assessment process was prolonged by the client's failure to complete a number of homework assignments despite an appearance of receptivity during the counselling sessions.

The direction of the career counselling took a different course when the counsellor, by chance, met Samuel's wife on the street after a counselling session. She indicated her frustration over the length of time that the counselling was taking. She stated that she had supported him through university and now wanted him to get on with job hunting so that she could quit her job and start a family.

This situation illustrates how the failure to adjust the field orientation to include direct input from Samuel's wife led to a complete misreading of the case dynamics. Samuel misrepresented the support he had from his wife and this was taken at face value by the counsellor. There was obviously a need to understand career decision making within the context of a troubled family. This led to a referral for family counselling and a more realistic involvement in career assessment activities. Because this case is somewhat unusual, it does highlight the importance of including significant others and making direct contact to substantiate information and impressions.

Situation 2: Time Frame

An employment counselling career reassessment program for professionals seemed to be very successful judging from the feedback obtained from participants and group leaders. After two intensive weeks of participation in the program, people reported that they had gained personal insight, confidence, an expanded support group, enhanced job-seeking skills, career direction, and a greater awareness of the labour market. Unfortunately these personal gains did not seem to translate into many jobs, and a success rate of 30% was all that was attained on completion of the program.

The conflicting information between outcome and process goals led to a reassessment of the data. Because the participants were professionals, it was perhaps unrealistic to expect immediate employment after the program. Also, many of the participants were engaged in career change moves such as setting up a new business, and this required additional time. A follow-up of the group members indicated that job-seeking behaviour remained at a high level over time and by 8 months the number of employed persons had climbed to 80%. There were also indications of greater job satisfaction.

The necessity of assessing outcome goals over a longer time period may be something that is becoming increasingly relevant in our current economic climate. Changing career direction is not easily done, particularly when people have to acquire additional training and explore entrepreneurial opportunities.

Situation 3: Goal Setting

Tara, a recent immigrant, was keen to find employment and asked for assistance from her employment counsellor. She agreed to complete several aptitude and interest tests, and her counsellor was pleased to note that she had considerable verbal and numerical ability. In terms of Holland codes, she was strongly oriented toward the Social and Artistic areas (SAE).

During the interpretation phase, Tara expressed her displeasure with how the assessment process was serving to limit rather than to expand her options. Her employment counsellor was somewhat confused by her reactions—wasn't the point of assessment to narrow options and to focus job search activity?

Further exploration revealed that from her perspective the overriding job search principle was opportunity not interest. She wanted to have access to all opportunities and was unwilling to set aside those that were not within the social and artistic parameters. In this instance, there was a misunderstanding at the beginning about the goals and the very nature of career assessment. Because this confusion was primarily the result of cultural differences with respect to values, assumptions, and general perceptions, it does highlight the importance of clarifying the career assessment process and goals.

Concluding Comments

The principles that have been outlined have a direct application to practical individual and programmatic assessment efforts. Following are brief summaries of some of the specific projects in which I have applied a broader career development perspective.

The career development of people who were unemployed was examined using retrospective interview accounts. These descriptions led to the development of several illustrative patterns of the emotional roller-coaster sequence associated with the unemployment experience (Amundson & Borgen, 1987; Borgen & Amundson, 1987).

In assessing the impact of job search groups interviews were conducted with participants three to five months after completion of the group. This extension helped illustrate how gains from the group experience were maintained over a period of time and also focused on factors that accounted for the success of the groups (Amundson & Borgen, 1988).

The effectiveness of a job search program with immigrants was assessed looking both at outcomes (employment, training, active job search) and the experience of participants in the program. A special effort was made in this assessment to contact people who had dropped out of the program as well as those who were successful in it. (Amundson, Firbank, Klein, & Poehnell, 1991).

The career development pathways of young people was assessed over an 18-month period following graduation from high school. By using a longitudinal approach, it was possible to assess emotional and cognitive shifts associated with the transitional process (Borgen, Amundson, & Tench, 1994).

Moving beyond the specific assessment efforts listed previously, all of which have certain strengths and weaknesses, it is important to emphasize that all assessment is limited by the approach that is taken with respect to a given topic. Data that are gathered will always reflect the starting assumptions and values that are founded in perspectives such as field orientation, time frame, and goal setting. The challenge of career development assessment is to be aware of these starting assumptions and values.

The choice of a particular assessment perspective is one that requires considerable attention to the value of the situation and to the self-structure. Choosing a perspective is often not a conscious decision but rather one in which factors such as tradition, personality style, self-interest, and situational variables play a major role. To move toward a comprehensive assessment, it is helpful to combine personal reflection with the use of several strategies and choose more than one perspective from which to view career development. The use of a variety of strategies helps to ensure a broader understanding of a situation.

Study Guide Questions

1. Using the image of a telephoto lens, how does movement closer to a situation (client) influence the nature and level of counsellor involvement?

2. Why is assessment of career actions over an extended period of time particularly helpful?

3. What is the difference between process and outcome goals?

4. Describe some key process goals.

PART THREE

CAREER COUNSELLING STRATEGIES

11

Career Pathways

Norman E. Amundson and Gray Poehnell

C areer Pathways is an individual self help or group program that offers a comprehensive approach to career exploration, assessment, decision making, and action planning based on the Centric Model discussed in chapter 6.

Some common questions and responses are put forward to help you evaluate the Career Pathways program:

How was Career Pathways developed?

The Career Pathways programs has been developed with the assistance of Human Resources Development Canada along with comments from numerous professionals in the field. Career Pathways has benefited also from the development work from other programs, such as Accessing the Labour Market (Amundson, Borgen, Westwood, Bailey, & Kovacs, 1992) and Setting New Career Pathways (Amundson and Poehnell, 1993).

The theoretical foundation for Career Pathways is the Centric Model of individual career counselling put forward by Amundson (1987, 1989, 1994; see chapter 6).

The first phase of the model focuses on readiness with particular attention to self esteem, expectations and basic needs. The first section of the program asks the question "Are you ready?" and utilizes three activities that parallel the first phase of the centric model.

The second phase of the model addresses assessment and exploration with respect to eight different dimensions. In the program this second phase is divided into two sections, the first focuses on the personal dimension with the question "Who are you?" This is followed by a career exploration section that addresses a related question, "What can you do?"

Moving to the third phase of the centric model, the focus shifts to the issues of evaluation, compromise, and integration. This is a period of goal setting and decision making and as such is the main focus of the fourth section of the program, which answers the question "Which career(s) should you pursue?"

The concluding phase of the model addresses issues such as commitment, action planning, follow through, and consequences. In the program this is addressed through the section looking at the question, "What can you do now?"

Movement through the various phases of the centric model is not necessarily linear and it is assumed that a person may move back and forth through the various levels. People following the program should assume a similar freedom in responding to the various activities. There may be times when it is important to revisit certain sections which had been completed earlier.

Is this a job search program?

When using Career Pathways, an employment counsellor should keep in mind the purpose behind this particular program. Primarily it addresses the issues of self re-assessment, career exploration, and decision making. While there is some mention of job search, this is not a main focus. For more specific information with respect to job search, people can be referred to additional resources or further programs.

Is it possible to add material?

There are any number of activities that could be added to the program. If activities are being added, it is important to keep in mind the overall length of time that is anticipated. Often when adding an activity, it is advisable to take something out so the process doesn't become overly burdensome. Also, in making substitutions and additions, keep in mind the reasons for the changes and take care to ensure that the flow is maintained. The infusion of new activities should be carefully monitored with respect to the overall process.

The assessment procedures that have been used in the program are qualitative and easily interpreted. If an employment counsellor should want to use some quantitative measures as a supplement, this could provide some additional information. However, with such revisions, it is important that the counsellor have the necessary qualifications to administer, analyze, and interpret the tests.

Do I have to use the whole program?

Career Pathways has been designed to serve as both a resource guide and a self-help program. With this in mind, an employment counsellor will want to ensure that the material selected fits with the particular phase of the career exploration process. The activities could be redundant or confusing if they are used at the wrong point in the process. Also, some activities assume that certain information has been gathered in previous sections; if sections have been adapted, the employment counsellor may need to help the person make the necessary adjustments in subsequent sections.

If Career Pathways is being used with people who are entering the workforce for the first time and have no work experience, they should feel free to bypass the first exercise and move directly to the second worksheet. The remaining exercises and activities are of relevance to everyone who is concerned with career exploration and assessment.

How long will it take to complete all the exercises?

The comprehensive nature of the program means that a person will have to devote some time and effort to complete all the material. The time required to complete a task will depend on both the ability and the level of motivation. Rather than handing the program to someone and expecting it to be completed in a week or two, it is often better to have the person work on selected portions as a homework assignment between meetings. Self study combined with guided exploration can serve to facilitate an expedient completion of the Career Pathways program.

When people complete similar activities using a group format, such as Setting New Career Pathways (Amundson and Poehnell, 1993), half-day sessions are conducted over a two-week period with the giving of a number of homework assignments

Who will benefit from this program?

Career Pathways is designed for people who are interested in reassessing their career direction and willing to invest some time and effort in this exploration. The activities are designed to have a wide range of application. People of different ages from various social and professional spheres should be able to benefit from part or all of the program.

In its initial development, Career Pathways was designed primarily for use with people who were experiencing unemployment. The program has proven itself to be effective within the unemployment context and also of relevance to people working with other client groups. In its current form the program is being used in government programs, schools, colleges, business, and by individuals.

Study Guide Questions

1. How does the Career Pathways program seek to provide a practical implementation of the Centric Model?

2. What factors should be taken into account when deciding whether to adapt the program or not? What issues should you consider if you need to shorten the program or if you need to add material to it?

3. What should you consider when you try to estimate the time required for a client to complete the program?

12

Cultural Bridging and Employment Counselling with Clients from Different Cultural Backgrounds

Norman E. Amundson, Marv Westwood and Rose Prefontaine

Editors' note: *While this article addresses counselling strategies within a cross-cultural context, the strategies described have broad application and can be used with a variety of clients.*

In today's global economy the issue of culture is very much at the forefront of any type of economic activity (Herr, 1993). Within our society we are also faced with cultural concerns as we seek to come to terms with one another. Cultural differences occur because of different life experiences. According to Sue and Sue (1990), "culture consists of all those things people have learned to do, believe, value, and enjoy. It is the totality of ideals, beliefs, skills, tools, customs, and institutions into which each member of a society is born" (p.34). Culture provides a particular perspective with respect to relationships with others, relationships with the environment and basic time orientation (Trompenaars, 1993). These perspectives provide a fertile ground for misunderstandings in dealings with one another.

The movement of people within and across societies is very much a reflection of our current situation . This transition is often accompanied by social, emotional, and economic challenges. For many immigrants and refugees the dislocation is considerable and requires a basic re-negotiation of identity within the new cultural group (Amundson, 1994).

This chapter is an adapted version of Amundson, N.E., Westwood, M., & Prefontaine, R. (1995). Cultural bridging and employment counselling with clients from different cultural backgrounds. *Canadian Journal of Counselling*, 29, 3, 206–213. Used by permission.

Faced with the above situation, employment counsellors are often one of the first sources of contact for the immigrant or refugee as they seek to establish themselves within the labour market. The purpose of this paper is to explore some of the ways in which employment counsellors can build relationships and intervene appropriately when working with clients from different cultural backgrounds.

Counselling Strategies

(a) The Beginning Relationship

The importance of the beginning relationship is critical. Gelso and Carter (1985) indicate that the establishment of the working relationship is the major factor that accounts for counselling success. Amundson (1993) points to the importance of "mattering" when working with persons who are unemployed. The concept of mattering refers to the sense of personal significance that we perceive in our relationships with others. Establishing a positive relationship with a client is regarded by various counselling theorist as a prerequisite for effective counselling practice (Egan, 1982; Amundson, 1989).

In a cross-cultural context the beginning relationship is developed through the recognition of cultural similarities, as well as differences. Pederson (1993) suggests that we need to keep one eye on the person and the other eye on the cultural context of the person during the counselling interview. By seeing the 'person' in the cultural context, we are more likely to recognize similarities between counsellor and client. Building the initial relationship depends on finding some common ground upon which to begin a discussion. It is a process of building a bridge between counsellor and client.

This initial information gathering and discussion must be based on respect, genuine interest, sensitivity, and an openness to new information. This process should take the form of casual talk rather than an interrogation. When a client's cultural background is acknowledged or interest expressed, the client begins to experience a sense of cultural and personal validation. Some illustrations of the types of questions that are appropriate to use during an interview are listed below:

• Tell me about your name? Does it have any significance within your family and culture?
• What country have you come from? What was life like for you there?

- How did you come to Canada? What was it like coming here? What is your current status?
- Do you have any family? Did you come with them? What do they think of what you are doing?
- Do you know what we do here? How do you think that we can help you?

In a recent three-day training workshop with employment counsellors, we found that a few counsellors were hesitant to ask these type of questions because they might be "too personal." While it is not difficult to imagine some situations where questioning could be "out of bounds," in most cases people are more than willing to share something of themselves with respect to their culture and personal story. If a counsellor is uncertain about asking a particular question, it is a simple matter of asking directly whether the client feels comfortable with the question. Also, by explaining how personal information can contribute to career planning, the client can have a broader context and rationale for the inquiry. Taking the time to ask some background questions helps convey respect, builds rapport, and establishes a foundation of "mattering."

(b) The Involvement of Family and Friends

Trompenaars (1993) highlights the importance of family and friends within the counselling context. An important step in building a relationship with a client is an understanding of the client's world in terms of significant others. It is often not possible to acknowledge the person without finding out about their immediate and extended family. This contrasts sharply with the individualism that is reflected in many North American relationships. In view of the potential significance of family and friends, it is important that employment counsellors make a special effort to understand family and friendship constellations.

Amundson (1984) describes a number of methods of involving family and/or friends in counselling. Perhaps the most widely-used method is the Significant Others Questionnaire. With this approach significant others are encouraged to complete a short questionnaire which focuses on the career talents and aspirations of the client. An illustration of this questionnaire is listed below. This particular form comes from the Starting Points group assessment program (Westwood, Amundson, Borgen, Bailey, & Davies, 1994).

Please complete the following questions. Your opinion is important to help make future career plans; therefore, your honestly is greatly appreciated.

1. What would you say this person is good at? What skills has this person demonstrated?
2. What would you see as this person's major interest areas?
3. How would you describe the personal characteristics of this person?
4. What positive changes have you noticed over time in this person, especially in relation to work or looking for work?
5. In what ways could this person continue to improve?
6. If you were to suggest the ideal job or career prospects for this person, what would it be?

Using the above questionnaire, of course, is only appropriate in situations where the significant others are able to communicate in English. In many cross-cultural situations this may not be the case and the counsellor will have to rely on discussions with the client about his/her family and social situation. As was mentioned above, these discussions provide valuable information and also help to establish the cultural bridge.

(c) Transferable Skills and Attitudes

As people move beyond the initial relationship, they will need to do some exploration of themselves (interests, values, skills, personality) and the labour market (Amundson & Poehnell, 1995). One of the most critical issues during this period is that of determining the transferable skills and attitudes. At one level the recognition of qualifications must be addressed, and the employment counsellor can play a major role in helping clients deal with various levels of bureaucracy. The task of gaining recognition for qualifications from another country can take time and the results are often not encouraging. Thus, the counsellor must also be prepared to help clients deal with disappointments associated with the process.

Beyond the formal qualification issue there is the task of translating past experiences into terms which are applicable within the local labour market. It is within this domain that the counsellor assumes the role of "cultural guide" and helps clients to find areas of overlap. Relevant skills and attitudes need to be identified and framed within a North American context. Achieving this goal requires a full exploration of clients stories, with careful attention to detail, and a focus upon identifying patterns of similarity.

The process of helping clients identify transferable skills and attitudes must be grounded in reality but also reflect a spirit of optimism. The best way to achieve this goal is to allow clients to express their fears and disappointments, to acknowledge the normalcy of these emotions, to recognize their strengths and assets, and finally to focus on realistic action planning which includes both short- and long- term goals.

(d) Behaviour Rehearsal

The role of "cultural guide" is very important as clients attempt to negotiate information and job interviews. There are many competencies associated with the interviewing and job maintenance process. When explaining this information to a client, it is relatively easy to overlook basic information. Some of the points with respect to interviewing that could be addressed include: a) timing of the interview; b) getting to the interview; c) clothing; d) going alone to the interview; e) body language, eye contact, hand shake; f) gender issues; g) the greeting of the receptionist and interviewer; h) where to sit and how; i) making casual conversation; j) answering questions in the interview; k) asking questions; 1) leaving the interview; and m) follow up actions.

Addressing the complexities of the interviewing process can be overwhelming for clients and is usually best approached through behaviour rehearsal. As a teaching and learning strategy, the advantages of demonstration and practice is well established (Mak, Westwood, & Ishiyama, 1994). Westwood (1994) has developed the following twelve step behaviour rehearsal process for teaching social-cultural competence:

1. **ASSESS**: use basic communication skills to determine needs of the client and assess what is the preferred approach.
2. **EXPLAIN**: outline why and how specific skills may be of help in achieving a goal and include some minimal cultural explanations for this.
3. **DEMONSTRATE** (1): show the client how to use the skill by demonstrating and modeling while the client observes.
4. **COMMENT & QUESTION**: encourage the client to discuss what happened and what they saw or heard. Clarify any areas of confusion.

5. **PRACTICE & COACH**: invite the client to try to repeat/simulate what was previously modelled. The client is now practising the behaviors while the leader assumes the stance of coach.
6. **FEEDBACK & ENCOURAGEMENT**: focus on the positive achievements and add correction where necessary.
7. **DEMONSTRATE** (2): show the client a second time how to use the skill through demonstration.
8. **COMMENT & COACH**: repeat as above with client discussing how to incorporate additional changes.
9. **PRACTICE & COACH**: repeat step number five.
10. **FEEDBACK & ENCOURAGEMENT**: repeat step number six.
11. **GOAL SETTING & CONTRACTING**: have the client practice the skill in an actual setting. Allow time for additional practice if necessary.
12. **FOLLOW-UP**: check on progress and provide additional encouragement and practice.

This comprehensive behaviour rehearsal strategy is designed to provide ample opportunity for illustration, practise, encouragement, and correction. The step-by-step competency development approach can best be explained through an illustration. The client in this case is an unemployed, professionally trained accountant from Hong Kong who has recently arrived in Canada and has made several attempts to get a job. He indicates that he has made it to the interview but seems to feel lost and uncertain as to how to present himself. He has tried on previous attempts to impress interviewers by bringing to the interview numerous documents to prove his ability. The counsellor recognizes that this client may not be aware of how to prepare and approach the actual interview. "Culturally appropriate" behaviours are reviewed by the counsellor and compared with what he has done in the past. The counsellor models with the client "how" to ask and answer questions, instructs him not to produce the documents unless asked for, encourages him not to "plead" with the interviewers, and so on. All of these activities are replaced with statements and behaviours which are more consistent with the Canadian labour market context. After modelling these new behaviours, the client practises with the counsellor until they are both satisfied with the level of readiness. The client is then encouraged to resume applying for jobs and to try out this new approach in an actual interview. A follow-up meeting is arranged after the client has had the opportunity to participate in a job interview. This follow-up meeting allows for review and additional practise. In this way the client is his/her own agent, but the counsellor acts as supporter and coach. Of course, job search competencies can also be taught and practised in a group context, increasing efficiency and consolidating learning within a group.

One aspect of the above procedure which is often overlooked is the necessity for follow-up. Despite the best intentions of the counsellor and client, there are many details which might be missed during an initial practice session. Because of these possible gaps, it is important to conduct a fairly extensive review and follow-up when a client has not been successful with an action plan This review allows for debriefing, re-coaching, and a further integration of the client's personal style with the skills that are being learned.

Training Issues

Our approach to training counsellors in the use of the above methods has involved a combination of personal awareness activities and skill practice. This approach emphasizes the importance of self-awareness as a foundation for the acquisition of skills. As counsellors become more aware of their own culture, they become better able to understand the cultural concerns of others and are better able to appreciate information about different cultural groups and clearly "bridge" what initially appears to be great differences.

For many counsellors, the initial expectation is that cross-cultural training involves a type of "dog and pony" show where different cultural groups explain the main facets of their culture. Armed with this information, counsellors feel that they will be better prepared to conduct their employment counselling interviews. While we have nothing against information about cultural groups, we do have a concern about its place within a general training program. If it is offered too early, it can lead to false sense of security and stereotyping. In a recent workshop one of the participants from Jamaica pointed out the superficiality and misleading nature of this type of information. He made the point that if he were to describe Jamaica, he would have to consider the lifestyles from the different parts of the island, also the issues of urban versus rural, poor versus wealthy, age, gender, and so on. A short summary might give a counsellor a glimpse of the culture, but it might also induce a false sense of knowing (i.e., "a little knowledge can be a deadly thing").

From our perspective, a central message in training is that every encounter with a client represents a cross-cultural experience (Pederson, 1991). People are unique and as was mentioned earlier, the task of the counsellor is to seek out some common ground of understanding. Information and communication skills can help us with this exploration, but in each instance we must begin anew with an openness to the person in front of us.

Conclusion

The strategies that have been highlighted in this paper represent a few key areas of involvement for employment counsellors when working with clients from different cultural backgrounds. It should be noted that the application of these strategies depends on the use of good communication skills, openness and sensitivity (both to oneself and to others).

In many respects this training builds on standard counsellor preparation and adds a cross-cultural awareness. It is our belief that cross-cultural preparation is a life work that depends on personal development and reflective professional practice.

Study Guide Questions

1. Describe the process of "bridging" with clients?

2. What steps can be taken to acquire more information about the inter-personal context (family and friends)?

3. Explain how a counsellor can assume the role of being a "cultural guide."

4. Describe Westwood's behaviour rehearsal process for teaching social-cultural competence.

5. Explain how every encounter with a client is a cross-cultural experience.

13

Supporting Clients Through A Change in Perspective

Norman E. Amundson

Offering support to clients can take many different forms. The most direct form of support involves financial assistance for educational training, relocation, child support and so on. For many years this type of direct financial support played a major role in employment counselling. With staff and program cutbacks in recent years, however, the availability of financial support has been severely restricted. Employment counsellors who have defined themselves primarily in terms of a direct financial assistance role have found themselves facing a loss of role identity. The statement "Without program dollars what can I do?" has become all too familiar.

While the current economic crisis has certainly affected the ability of employment counsellors to offer direct financial support, there is still much that can be done by supporting clients through a change in perspective (reframing). Many clients unnecessarily limit themselves through their view of themselves and/or the labour market. Various reframing strategies can be used by employment counsellors to facilitate a change in perspective. A brief overview of some of the strategies that have been found to be useful by employment counsellors will be presented. These strategies are organized along a temporal dimension (i.e., looking back, looking at the present, and looking ahead).

Looking Back

1. Normalization
The unemployment experience may lead to negative emotional experiences, negative thought patterns, and a downward shift in

---

This chapter is an adapted version of Amundson, N.E. (1996). Supporting clients through a change in perspective. *Journal of Employment Counseling.* Used by permission.

personal energy level (Borgen & Amundson, 1987). Because of the isolation and alienation that often is associated with unemployment, it is not unusual for people to feel that the emotional, cognitive and behavioural changes that are occurring are signs of something more severe (i.e., mental instability). Assuring people that their reactions are indeed normal and realistic given the circumstances is an important first step in the counselling process.

In providing the perspective of normalization to clients, a counsellor should take care to ensure that he/she is not patronizing; what is needed is simply an acknowledgement of the experience. One way of approaching this task is to introduce the client to information on the emotional roller coaster of unemployment (Amundson & Borgen, 1987a; Borgen & Amundson, 1987).

2. Accomplishments

One of the side effects of unemployment is that people begin to lose sight of their past accomplishments because of the stress that they are experiencing. As a result, their self confidence declines and they are less able to conduct career exploration or job search. To counteract this negative outlook, it is helpful to focus attention on accomplishments from leisure, educational, volunteer or employment experiences (Goldman, 1992). The highlighting of accomplishments is something that is often best done as a homework assignment. Clients can be asked to describe in detail several of their past accomplishments.

An area of accomplishment which is often overlooked is that of resolving past difficulties. For most people this is not the first time that they have faced a difficult situation. Clients need to be reminded in the telling of their stories that they have faced previous obstacles and have managed to overcome them through the application of problem solving skills and a positive attitude.

3. Transferable Skills and Attitudes

Imbedded within the accomplishments that are mentioned above are innumerable skills and attitudes which can be applied to career exploration and job search. The second part of the homework assignment is having clients identify the strengths that form the core of the various accomplishments (Bolles, 1996). Most people fail to see the full range of skills and attitudes within an experience and the counsellor can play a key role in assisting with this process. In offering this perspective, the counsellor should only offer opinions after the client has had an opportunity to conduct his/her own analysis.

Looking at the Present

4. Positive Affirmation

An important ingredient in the change process is the level of self confidence which clients can attain and maintain (McKay & Fanning, 1992). To achieve this end, counsellors must believe in the capacity of their clients and communicate this through word and deed. For example, in the phrasing of questions, it is helpful to start with the assumption that something positive has happened. Rather than asking, "did you do anything that worked?" it would be better to ask people to "describe some of the things that they did that have worked." Through this subtle change of phrase, counsellors are communicating the belief that successes have been realized and the only issue is the identification of the successes.

In adopting the above perspective, the inevitable question arises as to what to do in the situation where there have not been successes. The task of the counsellor is to help clients see positive glimpses, even in situations where there is a negative outcome. By closely examining the process rather than just the outcome, it is usually possible to identify some successful elements within experiences.

In addition to affirmation from the counsellor, it is often important for friends and family members to reaffirm their support. Structured homework activities can play an important role in assisting with this process. For example, as part of the career exploration process a questionnaire can be given by clients to significant others of their choosing. This questionnaire focuses on the identification of strengths and career options. The purpose of this activity is to gain the perspective of friends and family members and to encourage dialogue outside the counselling session which is affirming and encouraging.

5. Externalizing the Problem

A common experience for people who are unemployed is the feeling of personal responsibility for being out of work. Many clients blame themselves for losing their job and for each unsuccessful interview. This self-imposed burden serves little purpose and contributes to feelings of depression and low self esteem.

The counsellor can help with this particular misconception by having clients "externalize" problems and only take personal responsibility for those elements that are within their control (O'Hanlon & Weiner-Davis, 1989). By being aware of economic trends and the steps in the interviewing process, clients can begin to develop a more accurate assessment of their situation. A focus on process rather than outcome goals makes possible the realization of ongoing success.

The above intervention is based on situations where clients are taking responsibility for events that are out of their control. The opposite can also occur where clients do not take sufficient personal responsibility. When this is the case, everything is blamed on the "system" and bad luck. Countering this defensive reaction can be difficult and is facilitated through active listening and encouragement.

6. Limit Negative Thinking

Negative thinking by clients is a common occurrence and often a realistic appraisal of the situation. There are numerous occasions, however, when negative thinking is overdone and thus the need for limiting and/or reorientation (McKay & Fanning, 1992). When clients are trapped in negative thought patterns, the counsellor should be prepared to interrupt and break the cycle of negative thinking.

At times negative thinking can be very subtle and include a feeling of hopelessness. This is often expressed with the phrase "I can't do it." A useful reframing strategy is to have clients change "I can't" statements into "I won't" statements. This can be done in the context of ordinary conversation or it can be a structured activity. Clients can make a list of things that they "can't" and then through discussion and support examine ways in which some of the "can't" statements can be turned into "won't" statements. Through this change of phrase clients are acknowledging the power that they have in the situation. Rather than assuming a passive stance ("I can't"), they are adopting a more active position ("I won't"). From this active stance, they are in a better position to question and change some of the ideas which may be serving as unnecessary barriers in their employment search.

7. Information Giving

In many situations, problems that people face are complicated by a lack of accurate information. The counsellor can add a new perspective by providing relevant information and/or by teaching clients how to access the information through their own efforts (i.e., library research and information interviewing).

Another important source of information for clients is that provided through standardized and qualitative assessment methods (Savickas, 1992). In many instances this information serves primarily as a confirmation of aptitudes, interests, values, and personal style. There are times, however, when the information provides an opportunity to consider a new perspective. Assessment can be included within the individual counselling context provided that the counsellor has the necessary expertise. In some situations it may be appropriate to refer to assessment specialists for further testing and test interpretation.

8. Decision Making

The process of rational decision making can add a new dimension to difficult problems. There are a number of different decision-making strategies that can be utilized. A common one is simply to make a checklist of the advantages and disadvantages of a particular option. Another way to approach the task is to validate options in a sequential fashion using a set of established criteria. A comprehensive method is to use a career grid to compare options against various considerations. One or all of these methods may be utilized at various times to assess options. A rational approach to career decision making enables clients to effectively sort information and identify key issues which may be impeding their action planning.

While rational decision making offers certain advantages, it also has limitations. In the context of the current fast changing labour market, Gelatt (1989) suggests that it is more helpful to use a decision-making approach that is more intuitive and forward looking. This approach builds on the notion of making decisions in the midst of uncertainty.

Looking Ahead

9. Hypothetical Solutions

For most people the world looks much clearer when looking back rather than forward. It is often in retrospect that we can see most clearly the impact of our actions. One way of approximating this frame of mind, and thus attaining greater clarity, is to have clients imagine that they have attained their goal(s). Once they have visualized their accomplishments they can look back and specify the steps (actions) that needed to be taken in order to arrive at a successful resolution (Walter &

Peller, 1992). This change in perspective can often lead to a fresh understanding of the problem.

If clients have difficulty imagining the solution from their own perspective, they can be encouraged to report how others (the counsellor, a friend, a family member) will view the situation once it is resolved. Again, clients need to specify what happened to bring about the change.

10. Modeling/Rehearsal

As clients seek to come to terms with their situation, new behaviors may need to be learned. It is often helpful for the counsellor to illustrate what is required through demonstration and modeling as well as discussion. Many people learn more effectively through observation.

Clients also need to have the opportunity to rehearse or practice various actions. This process not only helps with action planning but can on occasion also lead to a new perspective of a situation. The rehearsal process can take place at two different levels. Often the first step is to mentally rehearse and imagine the specific details and actions prior to direct action. By imagining each of the various activities, clients can become better prepared for actual situations and may also attain some new insights. Along with rehearsal through mental imagery, clients may benefit from direct behavioural rehearsal. With the counsellor assuming the role of participant-coach, clients can practice roleplaying activities such as telephone contacts, information interviewing and job interviewing. This practice can be enhanced through audio and videotape facilities. The effectiveness of the rehearsal is crystallized through the use of constructive positive feedback. The purpose of rehearsal is not only to correct problems but also to build self confidence.

11. New Cycles of Activity

Clients often have established patterns of activity which are not helping them to reach their goals. These patterns need to be interrupted and new actions inserted. To accomplish this goal, counsellors should be prepared to suggest alternate homework activities which may require a behavioural change in frequency, timing, duration, or location (Cede & O'Hanlon, 1993). If the goals of counselling are to have clients become more active and self sufficient in their career planning and job search, activities must be organized throughout the counselling process which encourage and reinforce active involvement. These activities could include library research, calling employers, networking, responding to advertisements, and so on. By actively engaging in meaningful activity, with support, clients will gain confidence and will have a greater likelihood of persisting with career exploration and job search.

12. Focused Goal Statements

As clients express their wishes and difficulties, it is essential that counsellors help translate this information into both specific goal statements and steps for realizing the goals. This process helps to reduce the size of the problem as seen through the eyes of clients and also has a greater likelihood of success. The emphasis on success can be enhanced by having clients actively involved in the carrying out of action plans and the monitoring of progress from the very beginning of counselling (O'Hanlon & Weiner-Davis, 1989). It is important for people to believe that the situation is changing for the better. Clients can be sure of the changes that are happening because of their collaboration with the counsellor and because they are actively involved in observing, doing, and recording behavioural changes.

Concluding Comments

The twelve reframing strategies that have been briefly described represent a sampling of some of the ways in which employment counsellors can support clients by helping them attain new perspectives on themselves and the labour market. While these strategies are wide ranging, they are not meant to be an exhaustive list. In employment counsellor training through Human Resources Development Canada, counsellors are exposed to a variety of reframing strategies (the "tools" of the trade) and are encouraged to keep developing new strategies. The temporal focus on past, present, and future is one way that is used to help organize the various strategies (a tool belt). A counsellor is not expected to use all of the strategies with any one client but rather to be selective, depending on the parameters of the situation.

To assist counsellors in using some of the strategies a new career exploration workbook has been developed (Amundson and Poehnell, 1996). This workbook can be used in individual and group settings and includes the roller coaster of unemployment, a centric wheel for career exploration, suggestions for generating career options, and methods of career decision making and action planning.

Study Guide Questions

1. Employment counsellors have traditionally relied on their ability to provide direct financial assistance to clients. As budgets are reduced, how is the role identity of the employment counsellor affected?

2. Describe the reframing strategies that focus on the past (looking back)?

3. Describe the reframing strategies that focus on present?

4. Describe the reframing strategies that focus on the future (looking ahead)?

5. What are the expectations regarding the use of the reframing strategies with particular clients?

14

MYTHS, METAPHORS AND MOXIE: THE 3M'S OF CAREER COUNSELLING

Norman E. Amundson

The importance of "reframing" within career counselling is well established (Amundson, 1995a). The notion of reframing is based on a constructivist view of the perceptual process. Cade and O'Hanlon (1993) define reframing as the process whereby a counsellor "provides or encourages the development of a new or alternative frame or meaning to a situation (either directly or indirectly)" (p. 111). Clients who come for career counselling have usually tried some actions on their own initiative but have run into roadblocks and may be unsure how to continue (Amundson, 1995b). Within this context the career counsellor becomes involved with the client in a collaborative effort to reframe the situation and develop additional action plans.

The process of reframing within career counselling can proceed on several different levels. Many clients have expectations (myths) which need to be challenged and reformulated. Metaphors also can play an important part in the change process as counsellors attempt to provide alternate frames of reference. With regards to reframing behavioural action, the concept of "moxie" seems to hold some promise. The focus of this paper is upon the concepts of myth, metaphor, and moxie as they relate to reframing within career counselling.

Myths

Career myths have been defined as incorrect assumptions or beliefs about the career counselling process (Herring, 1990; Pinkney & Ramirez, 1985). These beliefs can be held by clients and/or counsellors

---

This chapter is an adapted version of Amundson, N.E. (1997). Myths, metaphors and moxie: The 3M's of career counseling. *Journal of Employment Counseling*. Used by permission.

and have an influence on actions at any stage within career counselling. To illustrate how myths emerge during the different phases of counselling, a four stage centric career counselling model will be used to consider several common career myths (Amundson, 1989).

The initial phase of career counselling (Relating) emphasizes readiness and the establishment of a positive working relationship. Perhaps the most basic myth that has to be addressed at this point is that of "hopelessness." In the current economy it is not uncommon for both clients and counsellors to become discouraged and feel that there is little point in doing anything. While the challenges are certainly very real, there still are advantages to doing career exploration and planning. Other myths focus on the roles associated with the client counsellor relationship. Counsellors must resist the role of "all knowing specialist" and present an alternate image of active collaboration. Clients must also realize that career counselling requires work on their part, there are no easy answers.

The second phase of career counselling (Investigating) focuses on career exploration and assessment with respect to both the personal and external domains. Within this phase clients are encouraged to set aside some of their myths about themselves and the labour market and to engage in meaningful exploration and assessment. To illustrate, many clients "sell themselves short" with respect to their skills and abilities. They also may be thinking too narrowly in terms of possible options (i.e., only considering courses shorter than six months). Through careful analysis (qualitative and quantitative) and the input from others (family, friends, the counsellor, contacts in the labour market), new possibilities may emerge.

During the third and fourth phases of career counselling (Synthesizing and Consolidating), there is a need to draw information together, evaluate the viability of the various options, and commit to action. This process requires evaluation, perhaps some compromises, integration, and action planning. Some career myths which appear during these phases can be encapsulated in the following short statements: a) once you make a career choice you are committed for life; b) the choice you make needs to be totally fulfilling; and c) successful career choices will guarantee a successful future. The concept of "positive uncertainty" as put forward by Gelatt (1989) challenges the core of these myths and presents an alternate framework which is more in accordance with current labour market realities.

Addressing career myths within the counselling process requires sensitivity and respect as well as critical analysis. Success in challenging beliefs depends upon a strong counselling relationship, communication skills, systematic career exploration, relevant information, and at times the development of new metaphors. It has been suggested by some authors (Stead & Watson, 1993) that all career myths need to be addressed prior to engaging in meaningful career counselling. While an early acknowledgement of career myths is desirable, the approach that is taken here is that myths need to be addressed as they emerge during the different phases of counselling.

Metaphors

Lakoff and Johnson (1980) indicate that "our ordinary conceptual system, in terms of which we both think and act, is fundamentally metaphorical in nature" (p. 3). They go on to describe the essence of metaphors as "understanding and experiencing one kind of thing in terms of another" (p.5). Metaphors are particularly useful in conceptualization and communication because of their ability to assemble complex information into relatively simple visual images (Rule, 1983). These visual images then form the basis for action.

The need to create new metaphors in response to changing realities is suggested by a number of career theorists. Herr, Amundson, and Borgen (1990), for example, call for increased flexibility as workers attempt to negotiate their sense of personal identity in the face of rapidly changing economic boundaries. Herr (1993) goes on to suggest that flexibility and the ability to develop new systems of metaphor will play a key role in successful coping within the growing global economy.

The importance of metaphors in the development of flexibility and creativity has been articulated by Combs and Freedman (1990):

Any single metaphor is a particular version of a particular part of the world. When people have only one metaphor for a situation, their creativity is limited. The more metaphors they have to choose from for a given situation, the more choice and flexibility they have in how to handle it. Finding multiple metaphors expands the realm of creativity. (p. 32)

Expanding and developing new metaphors is clearly a major reframing task for client and counsellor within career counselling. New metaphors have the capacity to change concepts of reality and suggest new ways of acting.

To begin, it is important for career counsellors to develop some understanding of the nature of metaphors and how they can be used within counselling. Turning first to the nature of metaphors, there are several ways in which they can be categorized. Lakoff and Johnson (1980) suggest that you can look at metaphors in terms of structure (one concept structured like another), orientation (spatial relations such as up-down, in-out), ontology (viewing ideas as entities), and metonomy (a piece becomes the whole). Another way of viewing metaphors is in terms of components such as the nature of interpersonal relationships, the degree of optimism, the sense of direction, the level of personal responsibility, and the indication of potency (Amundson, 1988).

Analyzing metaphors is best accomplished as a collaborative activity whereby clients and counsellors work together to develop understanding. As an illustration of how metaphors can be interpreted consider the situation where a client described her situation as "hopeless, there's just too many people at the table and not enough food to go around." Further discussion revealed that a few people at the table were getting more than their share while others sat by the side and waited for any crumbs to be dropped. The people giving out the food represented government and big business and she placed herself with those who were not receiving any food. This image contains within it a structural view of resource allocation (earning money) as comparable to being fed at a table. The orientation is one in which there is a clear distinction between "haves" and "have-nots". Looking at the components of the metaphor one is struck by the lack of optimism and hope for the future. Receiving resources is viewed as essentially a passive activity where some are given excessive portions while others watch and wait. There seems to be little connection between any of the people and the major feeling is one of helplessness. Exploring the various facets of the metaphor helped the client bring into focus how her current perceptions were serving to inhibit action and reinforce passivity. She realized that it may be possible to become more proactive and establish some positive connections with the people serving the food. As an extension of this more active approach, there was also a realization that it was possible to get up from the table and help herself in the kitchen (i.e., entrepreneurial activity). Through changing some aspects of the metaphor, she was able to perceive the situation in a new way and initiate appropriate action.

In choosing metaphors for analysis, the counsellor does not have to rely solely on expressions of present circumstances. It is also possible to work with images of the past, present, and future and to introduce images of action which will facilitate movement toward certain goals. Solution-focused theorists such as Walter and Peller (1992) describe a reframing strategy that depends on the construction of hypothetical solutions. Using a "miracle question" format, clients are encouraged to imagine that all their problems have been resolved. The focus then becomes, what they would be doing differently. Metaphors can be useful ways of capturing how situations have changed and also what would need to happen in order to arrive at a successful outcome.

Exploring metaphors can be accomplished by using only dialogue, but it can also be encouraged and in some ways enhanced, through the use of visual images (drawings) and discussion. Vahamottonen, Keskinen, and Parrila (1994), for example, describe a metaphorical drawing activity where clients are encouraged to visualize their current situation and describe future developments. Clients are given a large piece of paper with "the statement 'Me, here and now' written inside a circle in the center of the paper" (p.28). They are asked to draw whatever came to mind and to include the themes and persons that they felt were relevant to their situation. The results from this type of approach have been encouraging. While some clients were initially hesitant and doubtful about the strategy, the usefulness of the activity soon became evident.

The exploration of metaphors is a good foundation for developing self understanding and in many cases this process is sufficient to stimulate the development of new insights and action (reframing). It would be misleading, however, to suggest that the development of new metaphors is simply a matter of analysis. The counsellor has an important role to play in terms of extending existing metaphors, changing some aspects of metaphors, and in some cases, proposing entirely different metaphors. These reframing actions must be undertaken within a context of respect for the client and sensitivity to the conceptualizations of the client. To illustrate, a person who is not interested in sports will likely have little interest in hearing metaphors from the counsellor that are framed within a sporting framework. The client may, however, have an interest in quilt making and it is within this context that images need to be constructed. A broad base of knowledge can be extremely helpful to the counsellor in constructing appropriate metaphors.

The expression and encouragement of metaphors by clients and counsellors can lead to a very different type of encounter than is usually depicted within traditional counsellor training programs. While basic communication skills are still the foundation of the relationship, the focus of the discussion shifts to an exchange of stories, metaphors, and drawings. Combs and Freedman (1990) discuss the fact that metaphors are indirect and ambiguous and can be understood at different levels. Because of this "indirection," metaphors encourage more active involvement and participation by clients and counsellors. The mutual exchange of metaphors brings added energy into the relationship and serves to facilitate a true spirit of collaboration. Reframing occurs as clients develop and accept new images of themselves and the situation.

To conclude this discussion of metaphor, it is important to acknowledge that there are communication style differences and the use of metaphors may not always be appropriate. Some clients may be better suited to more direct communication and an emphasis on metaphors may prove to be confusing. Counsellors need to have the flexibility to adjust their style according to the demands of the situation.

Moxie

Reframing is not something that is restricted to self understanding; it also can directly focus on behavioural change. As I considered the type of action needed for effective job search and job maintenance in the current labour market, the slang term "moxie" came to mind. Chapman (1987) suggests that moxie involves courage, assertiveness, energy, "pizzazz," skills, competence and shrewdness. This combination of attributes and abilities seems to fit well with a competitive labour market where transferable skills, self marketing, entrepreneurial focus, and networking have become essential ingredients for success.

Many people have developed a sense of passivity with respect to their skills and relationships with others. While they may have skills and be willing to work hard, they are unaware of how to connect with others and obtain recognition for their special attributes and skills, either when looking for work or when on the job. This passive stance may be a reflection of personality, but it also can be a result of stress, loss, or a general lack of social awareness.

In addressing a lack of moxie, the counsellor may need to reframe actions by assuming the role of social-cultural guide and/or coach (Amundson, Westwood, & Prefontaine, 1995). Using the metaphor of "social-cultural guide," the role of the counsellor becomes one of listening and understanding the basic needs of clients and responding to these needs with appropriate information and learning experiences.

Under these conditions the counsellor is assumed to have some special knowledge of the existing conditions (labour market) and strategies for effective action (career exploration, job search). Clients are still expected to assume a certain level of responsibility, but the counsellor is willing to become more actively engaged in a structured learning process—a "learning strategy" (Bezanson, DeCoff and Stewart, 1985). This learning may require some coaching depending on the particulars of the situation. Westwood's (1994) method of developing social competencies seems well suited for this situation and the key steps are briefly listed below:

1. ASSESS. Determine basic client needs.
2. EXPLAIN. Provide information.
3. INITIAL DEMONSTRATION. Model appropriate actions.
4. DISCUSSION. Clarify areas of confusion.
5. PRACTICE. Client role plays new behaviors.
6. FEEDBACK/ENCOURAGEMENT. Focus on positive achievements and areas for correction.
7. REPEAT STEPS AS NEEDED. Practice and discussion.
8. GOAL SETTING AND CONTRACTING. Planning for implementation.
9. FOLLOW-UP. Check on progress and if needed, provide opportunities for additional practice.

The learning of social competencies can be applied in many situations. Cross-cultural or special-need clients are obvious choices for this type of learning strategy; but even without these challenges, many clients are in a position where they no longer understand the structure of the labour market because of the rapid level of social and economic change. Effective career counsellors need to be up-to-date with respect to changing conditions and have the necessary communication skills to structure a positive learning experience.

Having made the above argument with respect to the learning of "moxie," I think that it is also important to acknowledge individual differences and the reality that for some, the learning of proactive strategies will be more difficult. Under these conditions, the concept of "coactivity" put forward by Bridges (1994) may hold some promise. Coactivity is described as a form of collaborative proactivity where people are working together to meet their needs. For example, someone with great technical skills but lacking in moxie may form a working partnership with others who handle more of the entrepreneurial activities. These partnerships may be mutually beneficial. One of the roles of the career counsellor might be to facilitate these type of exchanges, perhaps through career exploration groups and arranging networking and mentoring opportunities.

Partnerships are of course, not necessarily going to work for everyone. Another strategy for increasing moxie is to have clients assume a more active managerial stance by using the metaphor of a business when considering their job search. Under these conditions the job seeker is the CEO and needs to establish a board of directors for the running of the company (i.e., carrying out job search activities) (Burton and Wedemeyer, 1991). The board of directors help set a direction, provide access to information and resources, and offer ongoing support and encouragement. Board directors are chosen for their special skills, unwavering support, and ability to provide constructive feedback.

Concluding Comments

Infusing the concepts of myth, metaphor, and moxie into career counselling has implications for both the practice and training of counsellors. Looking first at the structure of counselling sessions, one would notice an emphasis upon collaboration and understanding the perspectives of clients as revealed through stories and imagery. One would also notice a high level of activity and an emphasis upon creating a positive climate for learning. In formulating responses within this context, counsellors would be prepared to use a broad range of reframing strategies through each of the counselling phases. At times the reframing may focus on basic information, in other instances there would be a reliance on images that reflect activation, self worth, potency, relationships, responsibility, optimism and direction. Use of images would be coupled with the development of moxie through discussion and behavioural practice and rehearsal.

Training counsellors in this method would include standard communication skill training but also encourage the use of imagery in case conceptualization and feedback giving. Metaphoric case drawing can be effectively applied as a tool for case conceptualization in counselling supervision (Amundson, 1988; Stone & Amundson, 1989). Images that are generated through metaphoric case drawings help to create a focus for the discussion of client problems and the dynamics of the counselling relationship.

In order for counsellors to be credible in the demonstration of moxie, it is essential that they develop an understanding of the labour market and the written and unwritten rules. This awareness comes through critical reflection and a variety of life experiences. It also is connected to personal development and self confidence. As was stated earlier, moxie involves a combination of shrewdness, style and assertiveness.

In closing, it is perhaps appropriate to stress the importance of collaboration and a positive counselling relationship for the successful application of myths, metaphors and moxie. It is only upon a strong interpersonal foundation that these various forms of reframing can take hold.

Study Guide Questions

1. Describe some of the myths that emerge at each counselling phase?

2. How do Lakoff and Johnson (1980) categorize different metaphors?

3. What five categories does Amundson (1988) use to analyze metaphors?

4. Describe the metaphorical drawing activity that is used by Vahamettenen, Keskwen, and Parrila (1994).

5. In addition to analyzing metaphors, what strategies can counsellors use to work with metaphors in their counselling?

6. How can the use of metaphors in counselling change the nature of the interpersonal relationships between the counsellor and the client?

7. In what ways is "moxie" needed in our changing labour market?

8. What does it mean to describe the counselling role in terms of being a social-cultural guide or coach?

9. What does the term "coactivity" mean and how can this be used in counselling?

10. How can the metaphor of job seeking as a business be used to help clients develop moxie?

15

Pattern Identification Exercise

Norman E. Amundson

C areer exploration typically involves an investigation of personal factors such as interests, aptitudes, values, and personal style along with labour market considerations (Amundson, 1989). This investigation can require considerable time, particularly if each factor is investigated separately through the use of qualitative and/or standardized assessment measures. Given the time limitations of most counselling situations and the desire to use methods which are efficient and comprehensive, there is a growing need for new methods of career assessment (Eckert, 1993, Amundson, 1994). One such approach is the pattern identification exercise (PIE) which has been used effectively in both individual and group career counselling (Amundson & Cochran, 1984; Amundson & Stone, 1992). PIE starts with past experiences and through an in-depth questioning process seeks to identify personal patterns which are of relevance in establishing career pathways.

Discussion

The work of Young, Becker, and Pike (1970) in the field of rhetoric served as a starting point in the development of the PIE method. Their heuristic procedure for understanding situations involved a complex system of questioning based on the notion of exploration through varying perspectives. The guided inquiry procedure developed by Young, et al. (1970) served as the stimulus for the development of a structured questioning method (PIE) which could be utilized in career exploration.

The experiences which form the basis for the career exploration can come from any aspect of life. The basic assumption is that the experiences of each person are unique and that a detailed and careful

This chapter is an adapted version of Amundson, N.E. (1995c). Pattern Identification Exercise. *ERIC Digest*, EDD-CG-95-69, Greensboro, NC: ERIC/CASS. Used by permission.

examination of the experiences will reveal some common life patterns. To illustrate, a leisure activity such as playing tennis can be appreciated for its social elements, the physical activity, the opportunity for competition, or for some other reason. The way in which a person plays (the good times and the challenges) can reflect patterns with respect to motivation, planning, attitude, and self concept. Uncovering these patterns can reveal some important personal insights which have direct relevance to career choice, job search and job satisfaction.

The process of exploring experiences is undoubtedly as important as the questions that are used to stimulate discussion. The client is actively involved in the generation of information, the interpretation of meaning, and the application of new insights. A collaborative working relationship between counsellor and client must be maintained throughout (Gelso & Carter, 1985). The client is respected as the final authority in the identification of patterns. The counsellor has an opportunity to provide input, but this is always done in a tentative manner after the client has had a full opportunity to identify patterns.

The number of experiences to be analyzed can vary depending on motivation level and the amount of time available. Each analysis of a domain has the potential to add new patterns, but there also will be considerable overlap. An important aspect of this method is to appreciate how certain patterns of responding can be reflected in all aspects of life. The counsellor plays an important role in introducing the exercise, but the expectation is that the client will be able to work independently or with other people to conduct further analyses. The client is learning a method of inquiry as well as identifying particular patterns.

Steps in Conducting PIE

The Pattern Identification Exercise involves client and counsellor in a defined sequence of exploration. A considerable amount of information is generated prior to identifying patterns. It is often helpful for the counsellor to use a pad of paper to write down notes relevant to the exchange. If note taking is utilized, the note taking procedure should be discussed with the client and the client should have full access to the information.

Listed below are the steps of inquiry which characterize PIE (see Figure 15.1, A Visual Illustration of PIE):

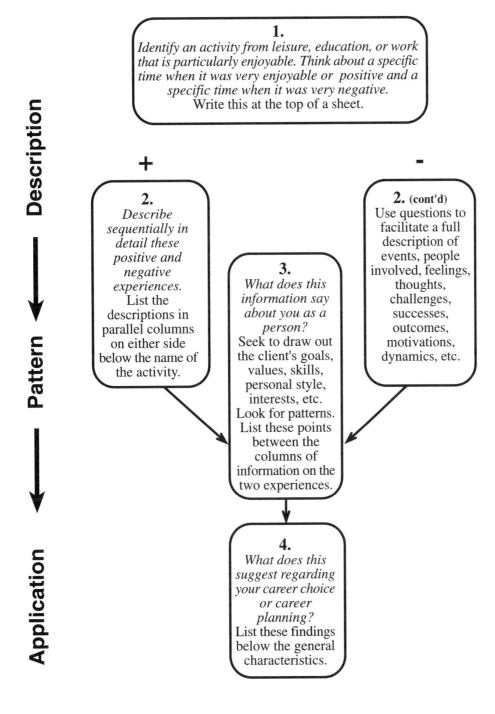

Figure 15.1
A Visual Illustration of PIE

1. Ask the client to think about some activity from leisure, education or work which is particularly enjoyable. Once a particular topic has been identified, ask the client to think about a specific time when it was very enjoyable and a time when it was less so.

2. Have the client sequentially describe in detail the positive and negative experiences. Some questions can be asked at this point to facilitate a full description of events. Ask about the people involved, feelings, thoughts, challenges, successes and motivations. What are the particular dynamics that differentiate the positive and negative dynamics? Depending on the situation, it may be helpful to extend the questioning to some of the contextual issues. Ask about how their interest developed over time and what they project for the future.

3. After a full discussion have the client consider what types of patterns are suggested by the information that has been generated. Give the client every opportunity to make connections and provide him/her with ongoing support and encouragement. Ask how each specific piece of information reflects something about the client (i.e., goals, values, aptitudes, personal style, interests).

    During this period the counsellor can provide some input. The statements from the counsellor should be tentative and be positively linked with client comments. While this can be an excellent opportunity for reframing, it is important to not lose sight of the client's contribution.

4. Connecting the above information and analysis to specific career themes can now be addressed. As above, the client speaks first and is then followed by the counsellor. The question here is how personal information relates to career choice and action planning.

As stated earlier, the above sequence of inquiry can be repeated for several activities. The counsellor serves as a guide for the analysis, but at some point the client should be encouraged to conduct their own independent inquiry (perhaps as a homework assignment).

In a group counselling context the counsellor would start by demonstrating the inquiry process with a member of the group. Participants would be then paired off and instructed to follow the steps of analysis with one another. The counsellor would serve as a consultant while the members discussed and analyzed their experiences. After a designated period of time, the group would come together for a debriefing.

Conclusion

PIE represents a comprehensive method of exploring career themes using experiences as the raw material for analysis. The process of exploration is client centred with the counsellor assuming a facilitative rather than "expert" stance. Through this mode of inquiry, the client identifies patterns of action which relate to goals, values, interests, aptitudes, and personal style.

There are several advantages to using the PIE approach for career exploration. The most obvious advantage is the fact that rather than initiating separate inquiries with respect to interests, values, and so on, it is possible to utilize one procedure. The inquiry that is conducted has credibility since it is based on life experiences with interpretation that is client validated. Clients through this approach are engaged in an activity which not only provides insights, but also teaches a procedure for ongoing analysis. Positive reports have been obtained from a wide range of clients. Comments often refer to the surprisingly potent nature of the activity. One limitation of the PIE method is its reliance on description and analysis by clients. The effectiveness of the procedure is somewhat dependent on the cognitive abilities of both the client and counsellor.

Study Guide Questions

1. What are some advantages of the pattern identification exercises?

2. What assumption about human experience allows this approach to be used with any type of situation (i.e. leisure, education, work)?

3. What type of relationship between client and counsellor is necessary for this exercise?

4. If this activity is used with a number of situations, what types of results might be anticipated and how could a counsellor work with this information?

5. Describe the four steps used in the pattern identification exercise.

16

A Cognitive Decision-Making Strategy

M. Lynne Bezanson, Carol A. DeCoff, and Norman R. Stewart

Editors' note: *As indicated by the author, the decision-making model presented here is highly cognitive and appropriate for many situations. More recently authors such as H.B. Gelatt have been expanding decision making to include other elements such as emotion, flexibility and imagination ("positive uncertainty"). A fuller description of this expanded approach to decision making can be obtained by referring to the Fundamental Counselling Theories text prepared by W. Schulz (1995) or by referring to publications by H. B. Gelatt (1989, 1991).*

Decisions are rarely easy or comfortable. They involve us emotionally and cognitively. A decision may look sensible but feel dreadful; it may feel right but be foolhardy from a logical perspective. The balance is not an easy one for the decider or for the counsellor attempting to assist clients to decide.

The decision-making strategy presented here is highly cognitive and is designed to assist people involved in difficult decisions to come closer to clear thinking and well-considered choices. There are dangers in presenting such a cognitive model. Some counsellors may see the cognitive process as a way to avoid dealing with the emotional content involved in most decisions. Others may see the process as too rational and dry, choose to deal exclusively with the emotional context, and not assist clients to sort out facts from feelings. A balanced integration is necessary for a counsellor to effectively assist clients in decisional conflict.

We are reminded of a story told by a lecturer who was faced with the decision of which of three countries to choose when emigrating

This chapter is an adapted version from Bezanson, M.L., DeCoff, C.A., & Stewart, N.R. (1985). *Individual employment counselling: An action based approach.* Toronto, Guidance Center. Used by permission.

from South Africa. He followed all the cognitive procedures we will outline here and carefully weighed the pros and cons of each alternative. The results were (a) USA; (b) England; (c) Canada. Happy with his decision, he went to bed and awoke the following morning, knowing he would come to Canada and he did! What happened? Did the cognitive model fail? Did the cognitive procedures sift through enough data for him that the decision suddenly made itself known? Would he have made the same decision without having tried to work carefully and logically at his choices? No one truly knows (including him) what happens at the actual moment of decision when one option can become crystal clear. It is known, however, that a cognitive process can *assist* in movement towards more effective decisions. It is with such a perspective that we ask you to approach this strategy. The strategy is also suitable for self-use and it would be beneficial to select a decision you are trying to make and to try out the techniques which will be presented. If you can make the techniques work for you, it will be easier for you to help clients use them.

Assumptions in Applying a Cognitive Decision-Making Strategy

The decision-making strategy we will be introducing to you is based on the following assumptions:

Decision making always contains the uncertain.

Many employment counsellors and clients approach employment counselling with the idea that decision making, particularly as it concerns vocational and career planning, is highly scientific and that the end product is an exact vocational or career plan. Clients should be aware that complete certainty in decision making is not possible. For example, it is common procedure in decision making to consider and evaluate alternatives and then to eliminate those that are impractical or not feasible. Often a good decision can be accomplished in this respect by a comparative approach in which the relating advantages and disadvantages of various plans are considered. This process will not yield a single perfect solution. On the contrary, a number of feasible alternatives are likely to result. Clients should be encouraged to pursue and experiment with several directions rather than latch on to a single, narrow goal.

There are no guarantees.

Neither random choice nor systematic deliberation guarantees that an individual will make the "best" decision for him/herself among the available options. The probability of arriving at the "best" decision increases through proceeding in a deliberate cognitive manner.

Decisions change.

Still other employment counsellors and clients approach employment counselling with the belief that decisions are made at a point in time and are final. Quite the opposite is true! Decision making is an ongoing process as is particularly evident within the domain of vocational and career counselling. Super's (1957) developmental self-concept theory of vocational behaviour, for example, views decisions as being made within the context of changes in life and changes in self-concept. There is also a present trend toward both job and occupational mobility (Toffler, 1970).

Too much information can inhibit decisions.

A sound information base is essential for effective decisions. At the same time, we have all experienced situations which frustrate us because there is just too much information to absorb. Buying one's first car is a case in point. One tends to read, look, test drive, consult with various friends, list advantages and disadvantages. At every turn, we are convinced that X is the best buy for very good reasons and also Y and Z are the best buys for very different but still very good reasons. At some point, we may find ourselves completely unable to fit together all available information and simply choose the one we like best for many wrong reasons. A slight exaggeration perhaps, but as counsellors assisting clients with decisions, it is important to recognize that too much information can be just as debilitating as too little information.

What to exclude is as important as what to include.

When facing decisions, it is important to recognize that one has alternatives—that options are open. At the same time, alternatives and options may be many; and it is not clear that the time and energy spent exploring all possible alternatives necessarily yields a better decision than time and energy spent exploring a few. Counsellors need to keep in mind that a frequent decision-making problem is what information to ignore rather than what to include.

The timing of the decision is often as crucial as the decision itself.

This can best be exemplified in the case of the individual who goes ahead and marries the "right" person but is not ready for marriage per se or the case of a person who buys the "perfect" house but the mortgage rates are unrealistically high for his/ her budget.

Decision-Making Strategy

Assuming that you have established a working connection with your client, then the counselling focus becomes one of:

- forming the decision;
- implementing (maintaining) the decision; and
- in many cases, re-deciding.

This is an over-simplified statement but it suggests the three main organizing points in the decision-making process.

In utilizing a decision-making strategy in employment counselling, two questions are of prime importance. First, which decision-making model is most feasible to use within the context of employment counselling? And, second, what specific counselling skills are appropriate and useful at different points in the decision-making process?

These steps provide counsellors and clients with an approach to decision making which can be readily understood and applied. Decisions, however, include more than the cognitive dimension. The effective counsellor using this approach assists the client to follow the steps and, at the same time, follows the client through his/her individual decision process.

Decision-Making Strategy Breakdown

Steps	*Guiding Questions*
1. Explain decision-making steps	Is my client ready for problem solving? Can my client define the problem as one of choice?
2. Determine if temporary action is needed	Does my client have the time to search? Does my client have an

		adequate information base for the decision?
3.	Implement temporary action	Does my client need an action plan to allow him/her time to explore and search?
4.	Generate alternatives	Have all alternatives known to both of us been identified?
5.	Determine appropriateness of alternatives	Have the pros and cons of each alternative been identified?
6.	Examine costs and benefits of remaining alternatives	Have the pros and cons of each remaining alternative been examined? Have the pros and cons examined included factors personal to my client: interests, values, practicalities, support systems?
7.	Make tentative choice	Has my client chosen the most promising alternative? Is it consistent with his/her interests, values, abilities and goals? Will environmental factors permit it to work?
8.	Complete decision process	Has my client developed a plan? Have steps been taken to maintain client commitment? Is my client well prepared to carry through the decision independently?

A client will frequently overlap steps and later backtrack to earlier steps. Some steps may be unnecessary for some clients and sometimes several steps may be accomplished simultaneously. The steps are a blueprint to provide structure and direction. You will notice while working through this strategy that the concept of "client-perceived risk" is important. Just as clients may be reluctant to trust and to change, they may be reluctant to decide for the same kinds of reasons—fears, insecurities, the unknown. As you study this strategy, recall what you have learned about reluctance and risk and begin to explore the application of these principles to decision-making.

Study Guide Questions

1. What assumptions can be applied to the cognitive decision-making strategy?

2. What are the three main organizing points in the cognitive decision-making process?

3. Describe the steps in the decision-making strategy?

4. To what extent is there room for overlap with the decision-making steps?

5. How does the concept of "client-perceived risk" relate to the decision-making strategy.

17

A Learning Strategy

M. Lynne Bezanson, Carol A. DeCoff, and Norman R. Stewart

Learning is more than acquiring knowledge. Learning includes developing skills, changing habit patterns, and discovering new ways of perceiving situations and viewing self. In an employment setting, clients frequently need help learning those things that will permit them to obtain and hold a job. They often have difficulty because they have failed to learn certain interpersonal skills, have failed to acquire persistence or self-discipline toward work tasks, or have failed to learn basic decision-making or information-seeking skills. Issues such as these can only be resolved by clients learning new and more effective ways to deal with these issues and by taking some responsibility for resolving their own difficulties. To be successful, counselling will have to bring about some lasting changes (successful learning) in the client or, at least, set into motion some activities which, if completed by the client, will lead to lasting changes. Employment counsellors can provide valuable help for clients concerning ways of initiating, responding, and behaving that will improve the likelihood of clients' finding and maintaining employment.

Learning, relearning, and unlearning are not usually quick processes; and it is not always feasible or possible for counsellors to be available and involved from beginning to end. However, counsellors can assist clients to develop a learning plan to acquire needed skills, habits and motivation, teach the plan to the client, assist the client in initiating the first steps in the plan and give the client encouragement, support and positive acknowledgement of accomplishments. Helping a client develop a learning plan to achieve an employment goal is itself a significant accomplishment. Problems often seem persistent only because no planned attack has been made on them. Even difficult problems yield to a planned and sustained effort.

This chapter is an adapted version from Bezanson, M.L., DeCoff, C.A., & Stewart, N.R. (1985). *Individual employment counselling: An action based approach*. Toronto, Guidance Center. Used by permission.

Regardless of the type of learning to be acquired, the following questions guide your interventions:

*   What will my client have to learn to get and keep a job?
*   What is the minimally acceptable level of learning to be accomplished in order for my client to get and keep a job?
*   What learning plan and learning experiences can we structure to facilitate my client's learning?

Counselling is a special form of learning. It differs from instruction in that it depends to a greater degree upon the client's willingness to be a central part of the planning. Client involvement and action are essential to learning within counselling. The solutions to the majority of problems presented by clients to employment counsellors require that clients be assisted to take action of some kind. The learning techniques to be presented in the learning strategy—Observation, Rehearsal and Feedback—are designed to assist clients to learn more effective ways of dealing with their existing concerns and to put these new ways into constructive practice (Cormier & Cormier, 1979). The techniques themselves are not difficult to understand. In fact, we have all used them repeatedly in our own learning efforts. Their practice and effective application within employment counselling is, however, a challenge.

Observation

Observation is a structured procedure by which a person learns through observing the behaviour of another person (or persons) who is able to perform adequately the desired behaviour. We all tend to do this intuitively and informally in daily living. We have all been in a situation where we have observed another person doing something particularly well. We have registered several things about that observation. One thought would have been "I'd like to be able to do as well as that." Another, "Exactly how did he/she do that?" We likely recorded a certain number of details and, without any specific planning, rehearsed in our minds ourselves doing it in a somewhat similar way in the future. This new way would be, according to our own standards, more effective than what we currently do. Informally, observational learning goes on constantly.

This same procedure applies to helping people, within counselling, to learn new and more effective ways of behaving. The difference is that in counselling, observation is carefully structured to bring about the precise learning a client requires. If the client is not already picking up new ways of handling situations from informal observation, he/she either doesn't recognize the need to learn a new way of dealing with a troubling situation; does not recognize that one can choose a different way of behaving; does not know who or what to observe; does not retain what is observed; or doesn't practice what has been observed. The counsellor role in structuring observational learning for clients is to ensure these conditions.

Observation proceeds in the following manner:

1. Ensure that the exact client behaviour which requires new learning or relearning is identified.

Precision is necessary in determining the core elements that require observation if change is to be achieved. This is most important in structuring learning experiences. A client whose goal is to stop being fired and who is instructed to observe the behaviour of someone who keeps a job is not likely to learn useful behavioural alternatives. The goal is too fuzzy and the observation too global.

However, a client who wants to learn better ways of handling criticism and can describe what he/she does now in response to criticism has a sufficiently precise goal and sufficient self-data for observation to be potentially useful and effective.

2. Help the client select an appropriate person to observe.

The selection of a model or models to observe is the key to effective observation. Negative learning occurs if a client closely observes and attempts to emulate a person who performs poorly. Conversely, there is some evidence to indicate that a flawless or perfect model selected for observation may be too threatening and intimidating. A client may observe such a model and become overly discouraged, having perceived that degree of mastery as being too beyond reach. The characteristics of an ideal model appear to be the following:

- Someone like the client, in age, sex, and background. That is, someone with whom the client can identify to some degree.
- Someone whom the client respects. The presence of respect is motivating when trying to imitate another's behaviour.

- Someone who is also perceived as "coping." That is, someone who performs the behaviour more effectively but still may make some mistakes, experience some nervousness and still be learning.

It is of course not always possible to find an ideal model. In exploring sources for models with clients, counsellors will wish to be attentive to the above criteria to the degree possible. In the example referenced earlier, a co-worker whom the client respects, who also receives critical feedback from the same boss but handles it with fewer negative results, would be an excellent model. The selection of a particular model will be dictated by the client's concern, goal, and individual characteristics. At the same time, the objective of observation is to find a model from whom the client can begin to learn alternative responses. There are several sources for models:

- **The Counsellor as Model.**
  In many cases, a counsellor may be a client's only source of an effective model. The client's home and work environment may not include other resources. When using the counsellor as model, the counsellor first engages in role reversal. That is, the counsellor plays the role of the client while the client plays the role of the significant other involved in the client's concern. For example, a client would be asked to play the critical boss as accurately as possible. The counsellor would instruct the client to carefully observe and note how he/she handles the criticism. Following the role-play, the client would be encouraged to discuss what had been observed, what the consequences were, and whether the counsellor's responses were an alternative which the client could consider learning to acquire. It is important to note that the behaviour a counsellor models is a suggestion to the client. Its intent is to show a constructive option, of which there are undoubtedly several. The client will need to adapt the observation to his/her own personality and situation.

- **Significant Others in the Client's Environment.**
  Counsellors frequently have a tendency to take too much upon themselves and not search for alternatives in the client's environment. Depending upon client's concerns, they can be encouraged to identify individuals in their family, work, or friend networks, who in their view, handle particular situations well. They may already know and admire someone who is assertive, handles criticism well, asks for assistance, has good work habits, etc. These

individuals may be more realistic models and more potent for the client than is feasible for a counsellor. Clients can be encouraged to observe such individuals carefully, to ask for their assistance, to engage in role reversals with them, and to practice alternative behaviours. Model sources outside the counsellor should be sought as often as possible. Counsellor time is saved but, more importantly, clients are placed in charge of their own learning and the learning is taking place in the client's real world. Retention of learning is therefore increased.

- **Other Models in the Client's Environment.**
  Clients can also be helped to find good models in strangers or people they do not know well; they can then observe them in an unobtrusive manner without asking permission. We can observe successful conversation initiators, for example, on the bus, during coffee break, in line ups at banks and cafeterias, and any other place where strangers mingle. There is no control over the quality of such models and the risk of negative learning is of course higher. At the same time, attentiveness to one's environment is a powerful source of learning and should be encouraged.

- **Symbolic Modelling.**
  In symbolic modelling, the model is presented through audio-visual methods—films, audio or videotapes, written materials, slide presentations. Several useful videos are available on the job interview which clients can be encouraged to observe for their particular learning needs. Videos are frequently used as observational material for assertiveness training. Counsellors are encouraged to make use of such aids as much as possible. Their effectiveness is dependent, to a considerable extent, on how well the client is prepared to observe and extract those portions relevant to his/her learning needs. A global instruction to observe how well someone else performs is not likely to lead to constructive learning.

3. *Structure the observation.*

Once a model has been selected, it is important to instruct the client on what to look for. Much time can be wasted by a client if the exact purposes for observing have not been carefully specified. Clients who report that they didn't see anyone facing stressful situations or couldn't find instances of anger being displayed obviously have not planned their observational experience well. Observing a person when no pressure exists or when no skill exhibition is necessary is time wasted. However, the product of careful planning can easily be the observation of a person responding or behaving appropriately under circumstances very similar to that experienced by the client.

Clients need to observe exactly what behaviour occurs during the event. For example, a person who responds calmly to harsh criticism may well exhibit a particular way of speaking or communicating non-verbally that contributes greatly to the general appearance of calmness. When the criticism is unleashed, we want our client to note carefully exactly how the recipient responds.

In addition, most of us are aware of the environmental cues that suggest the possibility, at least, of danger, wisecracks, scoldings, or happiness. The way a given person walks, looks about nervously, rubs his/her hands, or gestures may indicate what likely will follow. As we prepare clients for observation, we want them to note not only what the person does but also what has transpired immediately before. As the angry boss approached the employee, did he/she look down, turn away, move forward, or manage to smile? We want our observer to note carefully what happened first and how each party responded. An altered antecedent may greatly change what ensues.

Just as it is important to note precisely what occurred just before the event, so it is important to observe carefully how the model responded after the event. After taking a telephone order of great complexity, for example, did the clerk record all comments and file the order before accepting the next call? After the boss delivered his/her criticism, what exactly did the employee say, do, show? What else could be noted about the clerk's composure and apparent satisfaction following completion of the call? By focusing upon how a model acts and apparently feels after the event being observed, our client may get a better understanding of the satisfactions and rewards that come from having done a task well.

In structuring observation experiences with clients, we want them to be attentive to exactly what behaviours occur during, before and after the observation. They will need information on all three to look at and modify appropriately their own behaviours.

Rehearsal

Rehearsal, as the name implies, is a try-out, usually a series of repetitive try-outs until a goal behaviour is achieved. Rehearsal is the most frequently used learning technique. It also requires careful planning and is usually time-consuming. When individuals can learn what is needed through observation, this should be encouraged. In many instances, however, individuals will need both to observe and be guided in practice until they are able actually to perform the desired goal. In situations where the behaviour to be acquired is complex and generalized (that is, the difficulty is not just one boss and one incident but rather a general interfering behaviour) observation may not be sufficient. A certain amount may be learned by watching others, but the behaviour won't alter without guided and repeated practice. In planning rehearsal with clients, we need to carefully define with the client the adjustment in his/her way of feeling, thinking or behaving that needs modification, break down that adjustment into components when necessary, consider alternative forms of responding, provide goal practice experiences, and allow for sufficient rehearsal of the new or altered behaviours so that a client feels comfortable in using the desired way of responding. Rehearsal proceeds initially like observation but contains more steps as follows:

1. Identify responses needing practice.

As with observation, precision is necessary in determining what responses require practice if change is to be effected. Some behaviours are complex and will need to be broken down into graduated steps in order for clients to not be overwhelmed by what has to be learned. The example discussed earlier involved a client needing to learn a more effective response to a specific situation of receiving criticism. This behaviour in all likelihood need not be broken down but can be handled as a new global response to be acquired. A client who is shy, passive, and non-assertive and who needs to become more assertive to survive in a work setting may need to practice smaller steps. The client may need to learn to maintain eye contact, not stutter or stammer when responding, respond relatively quickly, and have non-verbal behaviours that are congruent with being more assertive. Counsellors need to be alert to breaking down a behaviour into its components when necessary for a client to begin to experience success and be motivated to continue to learn. This is frequently difficult as behaviours clients need to acquire may seem so natural and instinctive to counsellors that their components are not immediately obvious.

2. Select an appropriate model if necessary.

Frequently, modelling is a necessary prerequisite for rehearsal. The rationale for this is simple. If a client wants to do something differently but doesn't know how, it would be difficult to practice without a previous demonstration of how the behaviour should be performed. If on the other hand, a client knows how a behaviour should be performed but is unable to do it, he/she doesn't need a model but needs practice.

Where modelling is necessary, the counsellor would adopt the model role or explore with the client sources of appropriate models for this step in the learning process.

3. Provide and guide client practice.

Initial client practice of the behaviour to be acquired should occur in the safety of the counselling setting and within the security of the counselling relationship. Counsellors need to be imaginative in playing the necessary roles for practice to occur, in role reversals where appropriate and in repetitive modelling for clients when necessary. Providing the opportunity for and guiding and encouraging the practice are most important. At this point, counsellor support of the client may be more vital than at any other stage in counselling. If clients are to be successful in modifying social behaviour, extinguishing fears, acquiring new responses, they will need encouragement and success. Many of us have halted a learning process because we were initially unsuccessful and didn't like to face continued failure. We are particularly vulnerable when an observer can see our failure. For this reason, we want the first step in the learning process for the client to be a successful one. Start where the client is now and make the first step a small one. Provide support, coaching and positive verbal feedback.

4. Structure between-session practice.

Most of us have probably heard about (or perhaps been) a piano student who took a lesson each Tuesday and never had time to practice independently. Each subsequent Tuesday the student returned for more help from the piano teacher. Dollars were invested with negligible results. Practice between sessions is as important for clients as for piano students. But, just as the piano student has to have specific directions for practice, so a client needs to understand how time can be profitably invested between sessions. The nature of practice varies, of course, with the client and the reason for practice. A client who is very shy in interviews, for example, might be given a series of practice exercises such as continued observing of how others relate, attempting to relate to the stranger in a store or bus who seems "safest" to talk with, mentally practising how one could begin a conversation with a more imposing stranger, repeating the counsellor-client practice with a trusted friend, mentally reviewing the counsellor-client practice, and so on. Each practice should be directed at something that is agreeable to the client and is not overly threatening. It is much better that a client take a slower pace and practice than to be given difficult tasks and avoid practice. From our first work with a client, the importance of both mental rehearsal and actual practice between sessions is an expectation if we are to progress in counselling.

5. *Increase demands holding performance constant.*

Two concepts are jointly conveyed in this step. The first is that each step throughout rehearsal will be done well before a more difficult step is undertaken. The second concept is that we start with tasks that are perhaps very simple and lack the demands of the job world and gradually build more and more of the realities of our client's living and working existence into subsequent rehearsals. Although the complexity increases, the objective that, through repeated practice, the performance be eventually done well remains constant. Between-session practice should become progressively more demanding so that the client is gradually moving from performance in a safe simulated setting to performance in the actual environment in which the behaviour is needed.

6. *Continue increase until goal is reached.*

Our client's efforts in counselling would not be rewarding if the product of the practice fell short of the goal that the client and counsellor had set. Our rehearsals therefore need to be organized so that they eventually move our client from the beginning point of practice to a level that will serve him/her well in the world of work. Careful planning is necessary to ensure that sufficient time is available for engaging in repetitive practice at each level, yet the goal is eventually reached. If we know that a person is only likely to return once or twice, our efforts are greatly compromised. Inappropriate behaviours often take considerable time to acquire. Similarly, changes in skill or behaviour that a client may wish to make also take rehearsal time.

The counsellor can use three criteria proposed by Lazarus (1966) to determine when a practice attempt has been rehearsed satisfactorily.

- The client is able to demonstrate the behaviour without feeling anxious.
- The client's general demeanour supports the client's words.
- The client's words and actions would seem reasonable to an objective onlooker.

Feedback

Feedback is an important process by which we learn. Feedback is a way to observe and evaluate oneself and, under the right circumstances, to initiate corrective action (Melnick, 1973). Many of the important adjustments in our lives are made because of our skillful reading of the reactions of others and making adjustments accordingly. Sometimes individuals we care for and love will give us feedback which permits us to grow and strengthen our relationships.

Some clients have great difficulty in processing the information that others are sending or that may be stirring within them. In a job interview, an applicant makes a lengthy response and fails to note that the interviewer is yawning and looking at his watch, for example. In a job setting, a supervisor gives every non-verbal indication that he/she is extremely busy and the discussion with the employee has terminated. The employee keeps talking, oblivious to the cues. A person whose message system isn't delivering accurate messages concerning how he/she is performing could not be expected to improve his/her performance. The missing learning tool in this instance is accurate feedback.

In counselling, counsellors provide specific and constructive comments *(feedback)* to help the learner to know what is being done well and what needs further attention.

Whenever a client tries a new job, attempts to be more assertive in an interview, seeks clarification from a fellow worker, or works more independently, he/she understandably seeks to know how well it was done, how others reacted to it, and/or how satisfying the new experience is to the doer. We are concerned with the accuracy and helpfulness of the message that is recorded within our client's thinking and feeling. The message may be one of complete satisfaction, total failure, wonderment, or confusion. Whatever the message, we are primarily interested in whether or not it is accurate. In using observation or rehearsal techniques with clients, counsellor feedback would always be included as a reinforcement of new learning and attempts at learning. There are other instances in counselling where clients can benefit from counsellor feedback exclusive of other learning techniques. In order to use this principle, we help the client through use of the following steps:

1. Have client critique own performance.

If we are working with a client concern that can be or is being displayed in our office, we can rather easily determine the accuracy of the client's critique by observing the performance and then asking our client brief probing questions to help him/her evaluate the performance. Feedback that follows rehearsal provides a basis for recognizing successful performance, correcting problems encountered and finding out what our client is saying to self about his/her own performance. Frequently, clients are much too hard on themselves which places counsellors in an excellent position to be both supportive and correcting. Sometimes, they are not sufficiently critical and require constructive suggestions from counsellors to improve their own information processing.

Similarly, following observation, counsellors can readily ask clients to evaluate what they observed, how they observed, and what they retained from the observation. They can encourage clients to demonstrate what was seen which permits the counsellor to see the extent of their learning and the accuracy of their own assessment.

Many client concerns are, however, displayed on the job or in employment interviews and are not readily available to the counsellor. Creating an enactment of the event through a role-play or obtaining the client's report of what actually transpired are two possible ways of obtaining information when the actions take place elsewhere. Giving the client responsibility for a good part of the feedback begins to sensitize the client to his/her own behaviour. In order for clients to be able successfully to monitor their own learning, they must learn to be their own critics.

2. Reinforce positives following performance.

Whether we are present when the event takes place or must rely upon a verbal report or re-enactment, we can be very helpful to clients by identifying positive aspects of the performance. Regardless of how many flaws or deficiencies we might note, we can always find something that was done appropriately and we stress this initially. Clients sometimes incorrectly believe that no part of their performance is acceptable. We can give them confidence and increase their motivation by identifying positive elements.

3. Provide constructive comments following performance.

If all aspects of the performance were positive we would have no problem. Such is seldom the case. Clients are aware that they are not presenting themselves well, acting defensively, or being overly aggressive. However, they frequently aren't aware of the alternatives that are open to them. Understandably, they fear negative comments from a counsellor. Therefore, we can be much more helpful by providing specific constructive comments that suggest how they can do better another time. In providing constructive suggestions for improvement, it is important to be specific, to propose an alternative and to avoid overloading. A few specific points for improvement will be motivating; too much and too many may be debilitating.

4. Gradually shift feedback task to client.

As we work with clients, we want to encourage them to begin to identify positive aspects of their performance. This provides them with a form of self-reward. As they think of what they have done, they are pleased to find that they can accurately identify more and more aspects of their performance that are positive. For some this may be initially very difficult, but for most it is a fairly easy concept to master. Be certain to encourage their independence in looking for more and more positives that they can note. You will know that the feedback process is being successful when you recognize that, as a counsellor, you are gradually providing less and less praise and your client is providing more and more. Understandably, clients will experience reverses. Clients may have great difficulty in being constructive in their evaluation and some may not be very astute observers of their actions initially. Counsellors will then need to provide the positive and constructive commentary. With patience and consistent help, however, most clients can assume the self-feedback task effectively. The intent of effective feedback is to make the client more self-aware and more responsible for his/her own behaviour.

Study Guide Questions

1. How does the learning that is emphasized in counselling differ from instructional learning?

2. What steps can a counsellor take to help a client learn through observation?

3. Describe the steps in using rehearsal as a learning technique.

4. How can a counsellor use feedback strategies to promote learning?

5. What is the value of having clients develop a systematic learning plan?

18

Self-Management

M. Lynne Bezanson, Carol A. DeCoff, and Norman R. Stewart

S elf-management in counselling is a process in which clients direct their own behaviour change as much as possible using learning techniques combined into a strategy appropriate to their needs. In employment counselling strategies, most of the work directed towards the achievement of goals occurs during the counsellor-client interviews. In self-management, most of the work is done by the client between interviews.

Homework assignments are designed to place more responsibility on the client and by doing so, foster increased independence and client control. In the previous chapter, counsellors were encouraged to help clients identify models in their own environment, structure practice between sessions with significant others, and learn to provide their own accurate feedback. These are all methods by which clients are encouraged to take charge and to gradually need less and less counsellor intervention. In self-management, these same techniques are adapted and modified to place clients more quickly and more immediately in charge.

As you study the techniques relating to self-management, think of their double application to clients who can take charge immediately and to clients who are terminating counselling and need to maintain their new learning. The techniques to be learned in self-management are not entirely new. They are the techniques already acquired but applied with a more independent focus. In the earlier material on learning, emphasis was placed on the two techniques of Observation and Feedback. In Observation, clients were assisted to learn through observing others; in self-management, they are assisted to observe themselves. This is known as "Self-Monitoring." Feedback was presented as a counsellor-directed activity in which clients are provided with constructive

This chapter is an adapted version from Bezanson, M.L., DeCoff, C.A., & Stewart, N.R. (1985). *Individual employment counselling: An action based approach*. Toronto, Guidance Center. Used by permission.

comments and suggestions and assisted to begin to critique themselves; in self management, "Self-Reward" is built into client learning plans as a method of reinforcing and giving appropriate feedback to themselves. Throughout the previous discussion, emphasis was placed on breaking down learning into manageable steps that are achievable in a short period of time. This technique is expanded upon in this chapter as "Sequenced Learning," a method for clients to work through their own action plans. Self-contracting is discussed as well as techniques to help clients reduce negative thinking.

The advantages of self-management techniques are several:

- Use of self-management techniques may increase a client's perceived control over his/her environment. Perceived control often motivates clients to take action and also to persist toward goal attainment.
- Constant monitoring and reward are possible even when clients are alone.
- Thoughts and feelings as well as some behaviours can only be monitored by clients themselves. Counsellors have limited access, if any, to the client's day-to-day environment and are unable to be effective monitors.
- Clients learn techniques that they can use on their own with future difficulties.
- Self-management procedures assist clients to transfer what has been learned in counselling into their day-to-day environments.
- Self-management can be taught as a preventative strategy before problems arise. For example, anticipating problems that might occur on a next job and pre-planning how to deal with them may prevent the recurrence of a problem.

In self-management the counsellor is, more than in any other strategy, an educator and consultant. He/she teaches the techniques to clients, puts them in charge of their own change process, and is available to provide suggestions, encouragement, and assistance when required.

In order to successfully apply self-management, counsellors must feel comfortable giving clients as much responsibility as possible in each step of the employment counselling process. This requires counsellor behaviours such as:

- Not doing for clients what they can do for themselves.
- Expecting clients to be responsible.
- Not asking for more than clients are capable of, but not settling for much less either.
- Encouraging clients to take initiative.
- Verbally rewarding and reinforcing their positive efforts, resisting the temptation to "rescue" when clients flounder.

Self-Monitoring

Self-monitoring is a process in which clients observe and record their own specific behaviours or responses in specific situations. Obviously these behaviours or responses are in areas of concern for the client. Self-monitoring can be used in two ways:

- To get data on the extent of the problem for the client and thus assist in establishing goals for change.
- To keep track of the extent of the desired change once the self-management plan is in effect.

Self-monitoring is a useful technique to acquire this data for purposes of problem definition. Once defined and a plan for change put into effect, self-monitoring is useful to help clients monitor the extent to which they are reaching their goal behaviours. The very act of monitoring behaviours frequently brings about at least short-term changes in the behaviour being observed. The process of paying new attention to behaviours often begins to change them. For example, individuals who begin to monitor their cigarette smoking frequently find that they were unaware of how often or under what circumstances they smoke. The single act of observing and recording often results in their smoking less. The knowledge that behaviour is changing in the desired direction lets the individual know that the behaviour is, to a degree, controllable and encourages further efforts to change. Sometimes, self-monitoring is enough to get a client started on an independent change process.

Clients initially, however, must be trained as self-observers. They must know what behaviour to monitor and how to monitor it. Data should be collected on the behaviour itself, what precedes it and what follows it. For example, a client in a training period might record the actual daily amount of study time completed as well as what happened before and following successful study. In addition he/she might record the number of times study time was interrupted or not completed and what preceded and followed his/her behaviour. This provides client and counsellor with a baseline. Both know what is actually going on and realistic goal formulation become possible. With goal defined, self-monitoring would then continue in order to record the extent to which the goal can be attained without further intervention.

A method for accurately recording is necessary. The method should be easy, practical, and unobtrusive for the client. Notebooks and small diaries can be readily used. Small wrist counters are often effective. Whatever method is negotiated between counsellor and client, the method should result in the client readily being able to chart daily details of behaviour. It is usually better for clients to record behaviours immediately after they occur rather than to rely on memory. This is especially true with behaviours that occur several times a day and can be counted accurately only by recording them as they occur. Some responses of course occur much less often (study time for example) and would require recording only at the end of the day. Counsellors need to assist clients to develop a specific plan for keeping track of and recording relevant problem behaviours.

Once self-monitoring has been underway for a period of at least a week, counsellor and client should review the data, the trends, and tendencies it shows and decide together on the next step to be undertaken. If the client understands the data well and is making progress, no further intervention other than continued monitoring need be introduced. If goals need to be established, they can then be planned. If the client is misreading the data, it is important that this be corrected. Subsequent interviews need not be lengthy depending upon the progress of the client. A certain amount of feedback is useful, however, and encourages clients to continue.

The Use Of Self-Reward In Self-Management

During the learning phase, monitoring a new response may not automatically produce a positive consequence. Learners are often initially inept and their efforts do not immediately produce the results they want. Monitoring unproductive behaviours and realizing how often they interfere with progress may not be immediately rewarding; it is more likely immediately depressing. Learning to change a habit means giving up something that, for whatever reason, contained its own reward. Otherwise we wouldn't be doing it. The individual who is avoiding studying is somehow finding this behaviour rewarding. It is difficult to give up a reward for what initially may feel like a punishment. Counsellor use of feedback, encouragement and acknowledgement of client achievements is very important throughout self-management strategies. In addition, clients can be taught to reward themselves to encourage goal-directed efforts. Self-reward, when it is made contingent upon goal-directed behaviour, is a self-management technique. Individuals often need rewards to motivate self-improvement and must be able to not only monitor their own responses but also reward responses they determine to be goal directed. Self-monitoring and self-reward are very frequently used in combination in organizing a self-management strategy.

When clients are embarking on a strategy for change, explore with them how they plan to reward themselves for small steps achieved toward change. The counsellor role is to encourage clients to look at remarks which would be meaningful to them. The choice of reward and the determination of when it is deserved is up to the client.

Rewards can take several forms. The ones we most commonly think of are of course material rewards—a new dress in a smaller size after X number of pounds are lost or a special dinner after a particular job is completed. Material rewards are perhaps the easiest to think of and relate to, but they are not always either practical or the most effective. Rewards can be self-praise such as thinking or telling oneself "I did a good job." They can be postponing pleasurable activities routinely done such as relaxing to music, watching a favourite television program, bicycling, reading a favourite author or magazine until a certain amount of the goal activity has been successfully completed; what is rewarding differs from individual to individual. For this reason it is important that clients generate their own rewards. They can be assisted in doing this by exploring questions such as the following:

- What do you do for fun?
- What do you do to relax?
- What makes you feel good?
- Of the things you do everyday, which would you hate to give up?
- What are your hobbies?
- What people do you like to be with?
- What do you like to do with those people?

Client exploration of these issues will usually suggest areas the client can use as personal rewards. Counsellors can then assist clients to choose from these areas, an activity or activities which they could build into their action plans and "treat themselves" with when appropriate. Clients also usually need assistance in determining when is "appropriate." They should be helped to reward themselves for significant small steps rather then save a reward for full goal achievement. The latter is usually too distant to foster continued motivation. The involvement of significant others in the client's environment who will provide ongoing reinforcement of the client's progress should also be encouraged.

Built-in self-rewards in combination with a self-monitoring plan can assist clients, particularly during early change efforts, to remain motivated and to experience a degree of pleasure in their accomplishment. Self-rewards encourage positive steps which are initially experienced as difficult and non-rewarding.

Sequenced Learning

Sequenced learning is an arrangement of learning steps of manageable size which leads from things the client is now capable of doing to those things he/she will be able to do when the employment goal is reached. In the learning strategy chapter, behaviours to be observed and rehearsed were broken down into manageable steps, practice was conducted in situations of minimal threat and gradually switched to more real life situations. These are examples of sequenced learning applied in a counsellor-conducted strategy. In self-management, the exact same principles apply except that the client manages his/her learning steps more independently of the counsellor. These learning steps can be placed in contract form (self-contracting) as the client's blueprint for change.

Should a client not respond to sequenced learning and not be able to function independently, then the use of counsellor-assisted learning strategies would be continued. For the moment, we turn our attention to how we go about generating steps in sequenced learning.

A history of failure makes it difficult for some clients to learn new or modified responses. Minimizing the chance of failure and maximizing the probability of success is the key part of any learning experience. Success generates enthusiasm and continued effort, while failure leads to discouragement and abandonment Clients who pride themselves on self-sufficiency may find it very difficult to work closely with a counsellor and would be particularly good candidates for "going it on their own" with a sequenced learning strategy. To promote learning and minimize failure in using sequenced learning, the seven considerations that follow should be heeded:

1. Divide learning into manageable steps arranged in a sequence.
2. Make the first step one that the client can manage with little effort.
3. Make each succeeding step small enough so that the client can accomplish it but not so small that there is no sense of accomplishment.
4. Encourage the client to take the initiative in developing learning activities.
5. Make certain that the client understands clearly what is expected and whether or not the step has been completed.
6. Keep the goal clearly in mind throughout the development and implementation of the strategy.
7. Praise and encourage client progress.

Any one of the above steps might be chosen as an initial learning step depending upon what might be reasonably expected from the client. Other learning steps would then be arranged to build upon the initial experience. Each step involves progressively more action by the client and places him/her sequentially in a position which may be more personally threatening.

A number of common ways exist for arranging learning steps in a sequence. As you consider the use of sequenced learning as a self-management strategy with a client, you will want to consider which of the following holds the most promise.

Natural or Logical Sequences

Sometimes the ordering of steps is dictated by the nature of the activity. Obtaining a job application, filling it out, submitting it, and following it up with a phone call, for a simple example, must be done in that order. When arranging learning steps, help your client to look for a natural or logical order.

Sequences increasing in complexity.

If a complex skill is to be learned, a possible sequence of steps would be to encourage your client to begin with a very simple version or with one part of the skill and increase the elements gradually until it can be accomplished in its real-life complexity. One who cannot respond well to criticism might start by learning one improved response to a particular kind of criticism. The plan would call for gradually increasing the complexity of the situation until your client could effectively use a variety of responses to criticisms from a variety of sources.

Sequences increasing in frequency or duration.
Frequently the employment goal is not to learn something new but to do more often something one already knows how to do. A client may meet some work deadlines for example but not enough to satisfy a boss' standards. A client can be helped to increase the number of deadlines met and persist for progressively longer periods each day until an optimal time is reached.

Sequences decreasing in frequency or duration.
Self-defeating habitual responses can be reduced or eliminated through the use of a learning sequence that gradually decreases the time involved in these activities or decreases the frequency of their occurrence.

Sequences increasing in potential anxiety.
Learning things that produce anxiety can be sequenced so that initial learning and practice take place in a non-threatening situation, perhaps through rehearsal with a trusted friend. Later, situations holding progressively more potential threat may be attempted. For a client anxious about a job interview, practising first with a friend or spouse and later with other persons before going into the actual interview would be an example of this kind of learning sequence. The client's contribution is vital in helping to suggest and order the learning steps in ascending order of anxiety and difficulty.

Regardless of the way the steps are arranged in the sequenced learning self-management strategy, a client is given ample latitude to work at his/her own pace and is encouraged to consider alternative ways of improving the strategy. In working through the action plan, clients should clearly understand that their progress from step to step is dependent upon their successful completion of each previous step. This principle of advancement only after mastering more simple behaviours is a key to effecting change through sequenced learning.

Contracting
It is a simple procedure to formalize a sequenced learning plan of action into a client contract. In self-management, the terms of the contract are

specified and carried out primarily by the client, and so we refer to this as a self-contract. The value of self-contracting lies in its potential for strengthening a client's commitment to carry out action steps regularly and consistently. Having a written reminder of commitment promotes motivation.

A useful addition to self-contracting involves the co-operation of other individuals within a person's living and working environment when possible. Enlisting the services of others will both increase the likelihood that the contract will not be broken and increase motivation for reaching the goal.

The individual who has difficulty in meeting work deadlines and fears getting fired could be helped by a trusted co-worker who would agree to monitor inconspicuously but regularly and to provide verbal reinforcement and encouragement. A spouse can provide positive feedback for observed progress. Good self-contracts have the following basic features:

- The goal is clearly specified. Avoid the use of general statements, such as "work harder" or "call more often" and use instead statements such as "work for two or more hours" and "call at least every third day."
- The contract should be positive and include planned rewards for goal-directed behaviour.
- The contract should include a recording format that specifies the behaviour to be monitored.
- If the contract includes the participation of another person, the other person must clearly understand his/her role. A helper can be effectively used for modelling, monitoring, encouraging, and reinforcing. He/she should not be used to punish.
- The contract should be written. Placing the intent in writing encourages clarity of purpose. Signatures when another person is involved can also be helpful. It assists both to understand the contract's intent and accept the responsibilities that the contract specifies.

The counsellor provides encouragement and verbal reinforcement, as appropriate, during both the development and implementation of the self-contract. A time is usually specified for counsellor and client to review progress, revise content, if needed, and maintain the on-going consultative support.

Cognitive Self-Management Techniques

We have been discussing helping clients bring about changes in themselves. We have focused on changes in overt behaviours, but individuals also respond cognitively and emotionally to events in their lives. Thoughts, like feelings and attitudes, are private events not directly subject to objective verification. Nevertheless, they influence behaviour and are themselves amenable to change. We are concerned here with two kinds of internal response. First, there are the annoying or debilitating thoughts or feelings that are themselves responses to be changed. Second, we are concerned with deliberately-produced thoughts that may have positive influence on overt behaviours. Both techniques to be discussed can be incorporated into a learning strategy or can be taught to clients as part of a self-management strategy.

Clients frequently are not successful in carrying out plans of action, not because their motivation or will are questionable but because they do not believe they can succeed. Their self-perceptions are failure-laden and a small slip in achievement re-confirms their negative self-image. They may quit easily, not because they can't make it but because they believe they can't make it. Assisting clients to gain some control over their negative self-defeating thoughts may be an important addition to a self-management strategy.

Imagery

Vividly imagining how one would like to respond in a situation can provide a model for action. The imagined model may be based upon previous observations of others or remembered previous experiences in which ones own responses were effective. As you are reading this, stop for a moment and imagine how you would safely exit the building if there were a fire just outside of the door of the room that you are now in. In your imagination, you might construct several alternate models for action in such an emergency. Wouldn't having such models in advance help in an actual emergency?

Imagined models can be helpful in a variety of stressful situations. Imagining a coping model of ourselves faced with a sudden tragedy in our lives can be helpful should an actual tragedy be encountered. Rehearsing in our imaginations, images of ourselves coping in a relaxed competent manner in an anxiety producing situation can be strengthening.

A person anticipating some difficult social interaction can develop several models in his/her imagination and choose one to use in the actual situation. Many people use their imagination to escape problems; we are suggesting here that imagination be used creatively to help solve problems. Most of us have daydreamed and imagined ourselves as we would like to be. Often our fantasies are too unrealistic to be accomplished, but many individuals have been guided by more realistic self-projected models. Clients can learn to do this although you may need to challenge the client to engage in this type of activity by saying:

> *"Your imagination can be a potent source of assistance if you can focus it upon the positive goal that you want to accomplish. What you've decided to achieve truly is attainable. Think of yourself as having achieved it, how you will feel, what you will be doing."*

The object of using an imagined model is for the individual to have a clear picture of the response desired. Once the behaviour is clear in the imagination, it can be mentally rehearsed. The imagined response can be tried out mentally in a variety of settings. For example, an individual who is extremely anxious about a job interview can be helped to visualize a scene in which he/she is relaxed and feeling competent. The scene can be very remote from a job interview setting. It can be any situation involving social interaction—playing a game of tennis, enjoying an after-work drink with a colleague. The client can be helped to imagine how he/she behaves, appears, responds in as much detail as possible. Following practice with this image, the client can be helped to imagine him/herself in the actual job interview setting demonstrating some of the same relaxed competent behaviour. This latter image practised in imagination repeatedly can assist the client to demonstrate this image and experience less anxiety in the actual situation.

A specific response can also be imagined and practised mentally. A client concerned about his/her ability to resist the pressure of colleagues to drink at lunch hour can visualize how he/she wants to be able to handle the situation. This scene can be enacted in imagination repeatedly in preparation for the actual situation. Sometimes a client may have difficulty connecting with an image of self-behaving in a very different manner. An extremely non-assertive person may have difficulty initially conjuring an image of self as assertive. Imagining someone else in this role can then be a useful first step followed by gradually imagining oneself behaving somewhat similarly.

In such rehearsals in the imagination, one can try out various modifications of the modelled response and pose problems that might occur in an actual enactment of the response. Rehearsals in imagination allow responses to be practised that occur infrequently in an individual's life—asking for a raise, bringing a grievance to an employer's attention, apologizing for missing work, etc. Mental rehearsal allows one to practice responses that would require special settings or situations if rehearsals were to be actual rather than imagined. It permits the practice of potentially threatening responses in safety.

Rewards can be self-administered in imagination with a positive self-statement—"I've done well," "I'm making progress"—or a positive mental image or a feeling of well being. Many of our efforts are sustained because we have learned to feel good in accomplishing a task. However, some clients have not often experienced success and have seldom had occasion to self-reward or think positive self-thoughts. These clients can learn this kind of self-reward and use it to influence their own behaviour by deliberately thinking positive self-thoughts when successes have been achieved. They will learn it from you as you praise them for their accomplishment. In addition, you will need to encourage them to be self-congratulatory when they successfully achieve a step toward their goal. You can urge them, "Don't feel shy about being proud of your accomplishments. It's O.K. to think, I really did very well for a first attempt. You don't need to do everything right before rewarding yourself. Give yourself praise for trying and succeeding."

Effective use of imagery does assume that clients have a degree of comfort using their imaginations and that they can imagine situations in some detail. Some clients may go blank or be unable to describe anything beyond a skeletal image. With these clients, imagery will not be effective and a counsellor would switch to more counsellor directed approaches such as Observation and Rehearsal.

Changing Negative Self-Thoughts

Internal responses that are themselves targets for change are the negative self-defeating thoughts, the gloomy, pessimistic feelings, the unproductive, self-depreciating attitudes that interfere with the client's goal attainment. These internal responses can be reduced using a self-management program. "Thought stopping" is one technique that has been used successfully.

When a counsellor recognizes (and this is usually not difficult) that the client is consistently putting self down and anticipating failure, the client can be encouraged to verbalize what he/she is saying to self. Counsellor can assist clients to look at the self-defeating assumptions behind these negative feelings and explore more rational, positive coping substitute thoughts. With a coping thought identified and rehearsed in imagination, the counsellor would ask the client to think of the negative self-thought most likely to interfere with goal achievement. While the client concentrates on these thoughts the counsellor loudly says , "STOP!" This is practised several times with the client rather than the counsellor saying "STOP!" This sequence would again be repeated and when the counsellor says "STOP" the client would practise both stopping the negative thought and substituting an imagination the alternate coping thought. Following practice, the client would be instructed to do this at home several times a day and to use the technique whenever he/she begins to dwell on negative thoughts or feelings. Eventually the word, "STOP," would be simply thought rather than spoken aloud.

Structuring a planned diversion—something to do or to think about when pessimistic thoughts occur can also assist. Hobbies which require concentration—reading, serving, repair work, renovations and any others that demand full attention—are good substitutes. Remembering good times past or anticipating better times in the future can replace brooding or self-deprecation. It is worthwhile, although often difficult, to help your client generate a list of the positive things in his/her life to use to think about whenever negative thoughts occur. Once the alternative thoughts have been identified, some method will have to be selected to remind the client to abandon the old thought patterns and begin the new ones.

Summary

The techniques suggested in this chapter enable counsellors to train clients to become their own counsellors. They can also be used to help clients maintain and generalize their learning after counselling is completed. Self-monitoring is an excellent technique for acquiring a baseline on a problem-relevant behaviour. This assists in realistic goal setting. It is also used independently by clients to monitor their goal progress. Similarly, a self-monitoring plan can assist a client, following counselling to maintain progress. Self-reward promotes motivation and is frequently used, in combination with self-monitoring, as a self-management strategy. Self-reward transfers the feedback task fully to the client.

Sequenced learning and self-contracting are also frequently used in combination in a self-management strategy. They provide direction for client and foster increased commitment. Upon completion of counselling, self-contracting is again useful to place clients more firmly and confidently in charge of themselves.

The interfering self-defeating thoughts which often inhibit goal achievement can be reduced by effective use of imagery and thought-stopping worked into a self-management plan.

Using self-management techniques, clients are in control of the change process, and the counsellor serves as a consultant and a resource person. As emphasized, however, early in the counselling process it may not be possible for clients to assume full responsibility for progress, but such full responsibility is the goal of counselling. Self-management techniques provide opportunities, even in the initial stages of counselling for clients to make decisions and actively participate in the development of a self-improvement program. These opportunities should be used to help individuals begin to develop self-management skills. Increased client independence should be encouraged as counselling is continued. The flexibility of self-management techniques, to be used fully independently or to gradually promote independence is one of their clear advantages.

At the same time, discretion must be exercised so that we provide a clear understanding and don't leave clients with the feeling that they are being "rushed out the door" or pushed to independence before they are ready. Inappropriate use of the self-management strategy may result in various forms of client withdrawal, hostility, and rejection. As we have learned previously, it is best not to ignore these behaviours. Rather, we work directly to improve our relationship and shared understanding of our purposes in counselling in order that our clients can feel fully committed.

Study Guide Questions

1. What is the purpose of homework assignments from a self-management perspective?

2. What are some of the advantages of a self-management approach to counselling?

3. How can counsellors help clients develop their ability to monitor their own behaviours?

4. How can counsellors help clients learn to use self-rewards as part of the change process?

5. What are the steps involved in developing a sequenced learning plan?

6. What are the basic features of good self-contracts?

7. How can imagination and imagery be used to guide actions?

8. Describe how "thought stopping" can be used to cope with negative, self-defeating thoughts.

19

Strategies for Handling the Termination Phase of Counselling

M. Lynne Bezanson, Carol A. DeCoff, and Norman R. Stewart

There is always, in any type of counselling, a fine line between allowing, indeed encouraging, a degree of client dependency in order to promote the achievement of a goal and discouraging the continuation of this dependency after the goal has been achieved. This is of course why many counsellors have difficulty knowing how to end their client contacts. There can be a subtle type of resistance to ending a counselling endeavour which has been successful and a discomfort in not knowing how to do it without making the client feel in some way rejected. Clients may resist the end of counselling as well. If the counselling endeavour has been successful, the client has learned in a very supportive atmosphere which may be hard to give up.

In formalizing the end of counselling, the counsellor needs to be prepared to explain termination in a matter of fact way and to be alert to signs of resistance in both him/herself and the client. Counsellors need to be able to understand these feelings of hesitancy and to communicate to clients that they are now able to proceed without the counsellor's assistance. Since there are many other clients entitled to the time and assistance of an employment counsellor, counsellors need to be efficient in knowing when and how to terminate.

This process can be greatly assisted through helping the client to see that the learning in counselling has transfer value. The counsellor's final objective in employment counselling is to equip the client with techniques, skills and knowledge that will permit him/her to function in the future without assistance. Recalling the strategies we have discussed throughout this text, it can readily be seen that they have outside

This chapter is an adapted version from Bezanson, M.L., DeCoff, C.A., & Stewart, N.R. (1985). *Individual employment counselling: An action based approach*. Toronto, Guidance Center. Used by permission.

application. The steps involved in decision making can be applied to many types of decisions, not solely those which are employment-related.

The types of learning discussed—locating information, carefully defining problems and goals, observing, practising, giving oneself feedback, breaking learning into small sequenced steps—can all be applied to many types of learning. Clients often may not recognize this transfer value unless it is specifically pointed out.

Counsellors will need to discuss how the client can apply the behaviours learned to other situations and how they can obtain reinforcement when required from sources other than the counsellor.

In some instances, monitoring may not be appropriate or necessary. For example, if a client's goal was to decide between two training courses and the choice was made and implemented, there may be no need to follow-up. If the client's goal was to find a job in a specific field and he/she found it, similarly there may be no need to follow-up. If, however, the goal involved learning to be continued after counselling, monitoring can be a very powerful incentive to a client to continue to progress. Because of time and case load pressures, this is often neglected and understandably so. If it cannot be done with all clients on a regular basis, we strongly recommend that it be done with some. A quick phone call to check on progress; a 10-minute follow-up interview, and a very short note inquiring about progress may be a little time very well spent as all are efficient means of monitoring.

Record Keeping

Keeping written records for purposes of accountability (and counsellor recall) is vital. We recommend the following type of record recorded on index cards or on a copy of the counsellor-client contract:

Example:

Counsellor: _____

Client: _____

**Employment
Concern:**   1. Pending lay-off; re-employment necessary
                       2. Personally over-extended; worried about
                            finding another job

Counselling Goal:	Decide upon job option that enables her to meet financial commitments and keep up education.
Interviews:	1.5 hrs (3-30 minute sessions) Oct. 12; Oct. 17; Oct. 23
Follow-up:	25 minutes (1-15 minute session, Nov. 15, 2 phone calls)
Outcome:	October - Job search underway December - New job started Company - 4 day work week; possibility of 5 days in 6 months - reduction of some outside commitments
Counsellor Comments:	No further follow-up anticipated. Client managing well independently.

You may wish to add different details in your own record keeping, those you would find most useful to you. The above is a suggestion only. Note, however, that whatever type of written record you choose to keep, it should contain the following five essential pieces of information:

- Client identification
- What was the concern?
- What was the goal?
- What were the outcomes?
- How much counselling time did it take to achieve the outcomes?

In this way, you will have a permanent record of concrete counselling achievements recorded in a consistent manner and accessible.

Evaluate Counsellor Performance

The final step in the termination process is that of looking as objectively as possible at one's own counselling performance. The process of evaluation is, of course, an ongoing process throughout your working relationships with clients. You will, in working with the system, be asking yourself continually: How am I doing with this client? Are we making progress? Are we moving ahead as we should be? Are we working as time efficiently as we can? Are my counselling skills adequate for the needs of my client?

You will be making adjustment and corrections as needed. It is also useful to set aside a formalized period of time (it need not be long) to reflect on your total performance.

In essence, after closing a case, you need feedback on two important areas:

- How effectively and efficiently did I work with this client?
- What can I learn from this counselling experience to help me work more effectively with future clients?

Obviously, the immediate criterion for successful counsellor performance is whether or not the client has achieved the mutually agreed upon employment counselling goal. Taken alone, however, this does relatively little to improve your performance with future clients. It is conceivable that, given a co-operative and long-suffering client, almost any counsellor, using almost any technique, can eventually effect some desired change in a client's behaviour. This measure ignores economy and efficiency and deals only with results.

The counsellor therefore must ponder additional considerations and seek answers which touch on Quantity, Quality, Time Frame, and Counselling Strategies employed.

Consider the following as a guide to your self-evaluation:

Quantity Considerations

- What were the measurable outcomes of working with this client? (i.e., Job Placement, Training Placement)

- Were these the outcomes we planned?

- If not, can I explain why they were only partially achieved or not at all achieved?

- Can I plan to do something different next time based on this experience?

Quality Considerations

- What were the not-so-measurable achievements of my client? (i.e., Increased confidence; better self-expression; willingness to experiment; reduced anger, etc.)

- Were these achievements in my counselling plan to help this client?

- Did I use/forget to use any specific skills which I want to remember in working with this concern in the future?

Time Frame

- How much time did I spend in total with this client?

- Could we have achieved the outcomes more quickly?

- If so, how?

Counselling Strategies

- Did I follow the steps of the counselling system (RISC, see Chapter 6, The centric model for individual career counselling)?

- If I deviated from the steps, were my deviations justified?

- Did I use the most effective strategy for working with this particular problem?

- Are there specific techniques/strategies I would like to try in the future?

Without taking time to reflect on our progress and our "to be improved" areas, it is very easy to become stagnant and stop growing as more effective counsellors. There are three major sources of feedback on your progress.

1. Your own experience

The first is your own experience and your reflection and learning based on that experience. The series of self-evaluation questions just listed will serve as a useful guide to tapping your experience as a learning source.

2. Your client

The second major source of feedback is your client. Quite obviously, the client has the most immediate stake in the counsellor's performance and is especially qualified to provide valuable feedback. The client knows better than anyone else how the counsellor's techniques were perceived, whether the explanation of the counselling relationship was understood, whether the client felt that the goal to be achieved belonged to him/her, whether the tasks assigned were manageable and whether the client would be willing to return to the counsellor. At opportune times during or after an interview or upon completion of a case, the counsellor can seek such information from the client through direct questioning. The expressed reactions of the client can provide important indications of satisfaction and progress.

3. Qualified others

The third major source is. of course, qualified others—your counsellor colleagues, supervisors, and trainees. It is possible and desirable to enlist the help of others in the evaluation of one's own counselling. Taping interviews with the client's permission and listening to the interview with a colleague whose judgement and skill you respect is one of the best sources of constant learning. Sharing strategies, discovering more time efficient ways of assisting clients with similar concerns, sharing frustrations and seeking advice are strongly encouraged. In addition, referring to your written records can be very useful. If you have taken a few moments to record what you learned from one counselling experience and what you want to remember for the next, you have a reminder for when the next occurs. You can check whether you were able to apply what you hoped to apply. You can self-monitor to see if you can reach similar outcomes within shorter counselling time frames.

As a counsellor, one should be accountable to one's employer and the public for the quality of one's performances in terms of counselling and for the quantity of one's results. The first step of accountability is to be accountable to ourselves. To do so effectively, one must use the evaluation resources which are available and which promote increased competency, efficiency, and personal satisfaction.

Study Guide Questions

1. The termination phase of counselling brings with it certain feelings as well as opportunities for the transfer of learning. How can counsellors best facilitate this process?

2. What points need to be addressed in keeping a record of the counselling outcome?

3. What areas of feedback need to be reflected upon at the conclusion of counselling?

Postscript

Norman E. Amundson, Gray Poehnell, and Stuart Smithson

The articles that have been included in this book of readings point toward some important issues in counsellor training and development. The next step is having the opportunity to support this theoretical learning through an experiential counsellor training process (Amundson, Smithson, Thiessen, & Poehnell, 1996). These two elements taken together form the basis for the revised Individual Employment Counsellor Training program for Human Resources Development Canada (HRDC).

The expectation from this training, or other similar training, is that you will acquire additional skills for individual employment counselling that will enhance the basic skills and theories obtained through earlier training, such as Individual Counselling Assessment and Career Counselling Theories. To fully realize this capacity, however, you will need to ensure that you have the opportunity to use the skills that you have learned. In too many cases, people complete the training process, but then go on to other activities which do not include individual career counselling. As with any set of skills, a lack of usage will over time serve to undermine any learning that has taken place. Thus, an important task to consolidate learning is to ensure that you have the opportunity to use the skills that you have acquired.

Further learning within the individual employment counselling domain is also important. The ideas and models that are presented here are not meant to be the "final words" in terms of individual employment counselling. Continued exploration and learning is essential. The counselling model that has been presented is a basic structure upon which numerous counselling strategies can be placed. What has been covered is only a sampling of the possibilities. Continued learning and development must be undertaken through professional development activities and conferences to stay current and to further skill development in this area.

Expanding the focus of learning beyond individual employment counselling is another task to consider. While there will be some overlap with other areas, there are important additional skills to be learned by seeking training opportunities in group counselling, consultation, assessment, program development, and so on. You will be able to apply some of the skills that you have learned in individual employment counselling to help you determine the nature and sequence of additional learning that best suits your personal objectives.

Ongoing professional development is an essential ingredient in today's workplace. Involvement in these activities requires personal initiative and support from the organization. In addition, many people find it helpful to join a professional association for accreditation purposes and for exposure to regular learning opportunities. The active pursuit of learning will ensure that you remain effective and competitive in the market place.

Bibliography

Adler, A. (1939). *Social interest*. New York: Putnam.

Ainsworth, M.D.S. (1989). Attachments beyond infancy. *American Psychology*, 44, 709–716.

Amhiem, R. (1969*). Visual thinking*. London: Faber and Faber.

Amundson, N.E. (1984). Career counselling with primary group involvement. *Canadian Counsellor*, 18, 180–183.

Amundson. N.E. (1987). A visual means of organizing career information. *Journal of Employment Counseling,* 24, 2–7.

Amundson, N.E. (1988). The use of metaphor and drawings in case conceptualization, *Journal of Counseling and Development*, 66, 391–393.

Amundson, N.E. (1989). A model of individual career counseling, *Journal of Employment Counseling*, 26, 132–138.

Amundson, N.E. (1989b). *Individual style survey*. Edmonton, Alberta: Psychometrics Canada.

Amundson, N.E. (1993). Mattering: A foundation for employment counseling and training. *Journal of Employment Counseling,* 30, 146–152.

Amundson, N.E. (1994b). Perspectives for assessing career development. *Journal of Employment Counseling*, 31, 147–154.

Amundson, N.E. (1995a). An interactive model of career decision making. *Journal of Employment Counseling*, 32, 11–21.

Amundson, N.E. (1995b). Action planning through the phases of counseling. *Journal of Employment Counseling*, 32, 147–153.

Amundson, N.E. (1995c). Pattern identification exercise. *ERIC Digest*, EDD-CG-95-69, Greensboro, NC: ERIC/CASS.

Amundson, N.E. (1995d). The centric model for individual employment counselling. Unpublished manuscript. Vancouver: University of British Columbia.

Amundson, N.E. (1996a). Supporting clients through a change in perspective. *Journal of Employment Counseling*,33,155-162.

Amundson, N.E. (1997b). Myths, metaphors and moxie: The 3M's of career counseling. *Journal of Employment Counseling*, 34, 76-84.

Amundson, N.E., & Borgen, W.A. (1982). The dynamics of unemployment: Job loss and job search. *The Personnel and Guidance Journal*, 60, 562–564.

Amundson, N.E., & Borgen. W.A. (1987a). *At the controls: Charting your course through unemployment*. Toronto: Nelson Canada.

Amundson, N.E., & Borgen, W.A. (1987b). Coping with unemployment: What helps and what hinders. *Journal of Employment Counseling*, 24, 97–106.

Amundson, N.E., & Borgen, W.A. (1988). Factors that help and hinder in group employment counseling. *Journal of Employment Counseling*, 25, 104–114.

Amundson, N.E., Borgen, W.A., & Tench, E. (in press). Counselling and the role of personality and intelligence. In D. K. Saklofske & M. Zeidner (Eds.), *International handbook of personality and intelligence*. New York: Plenum.

Amundson, N.E., Borgen, W.A., & Westwood, M.J. (1990). Group employment counseling in Canada. *Journal of Employment Counseling*, 27, 181–190.

Amundson, N.E., Borgen, W.A., Westwood, M., Bailey, B., & Kovacs, S. (1992). *Accessing the labor market*. Vancouver: Employment and Immigration Canada.

Amundson, N.E., & Cochran, L. (1984). Analyzing experiences using an adaptation of an heuristic model. *Canadian Counsellor*, 18, 183–186.

Amundson, N.E., Firbank, O., Klein, H., & Poehnell, G. (1991). Job link: An employment counseling program for immigrants. *Journal of Employment Counseling, 28*, 167–176.

Amundson, N.E., & Kenney, S. (1979). The non-voluntary client. Unpublished Manuscript. Vancouver: University of British Columbia.

Amundson, N.E., & Poehnell, G. (1993). *Setting new career pathways*. Ottawa: Employment and Immigration Canada.

Amundson, N.E., & Poehnell, G. (1996). *Career pathways* (2nd ed.). Richmond, B.C.: Ergon Communications.

Amundson, N.E., Smithson, S., Thiessen, V., & Poehnell, G. (1996). *Individual employment counselling* (Rev. ed). Ottawa: Human Resources Development Canada.

Amundson, N.E., & Stone, D. (1992). *VanCity career development program.* Vancouver: VanCity Credit Union.

Amundson, N.E., Westwood, M., & Prefontaine, R. (1995). Cultural bridging and employment counselling with clients from different cultural backgrounds. *Canadian Journal of Counselling,* 29 (3), 206–213.

Anderson, S.M. (1987). The role of cultural assumptions in self-concept development. In K. Yardley & T. Honess (Eds.), *Self and Identity: Psychosocial Perspectives.* Toronto: John Wiley.

Bandura, A. (1986). The explanatory and predictive scope of self efficacy theory. *Journal of Social and Clinical Psychology,* 4, 359–373.

Betz, N.E., & Hackett, G. (1987). Concept of agency in educational and career development. *Journal of Counseling Psychology,* 34, 299–308.

Bezanson, M.L., DeCoff, C.A., & Stewart, N.R. (1985). *Individual employment counselling: An action based approach.* Toronto, Guidance Center.

Bolles, R.N. (1996). *The 1996 what color is your parachute.* Berkeley, CA: Ten Speed Press.

Booth, J.A., Begin, L., & Lavallee, L. (1980). *Technical manual for the Canadian Occupational Interest Inventory* (1st ed.). Ottawa: Employment and Immigration Canada.

Borgen, W.A. (1993). Marketing in group employment counselling. Unpublished manuscript. Vancouver: University of British Columbia.

Borgen, W.A., & Amundson, N.E. (1992). *The competence maintenance project: Final report.* Edmonton: Employment and Immigration Canada.

Borgen. W.A., & Amundson. N.E. (1987). The dynamics of unemployment. *Journal of Counseling and Development,* 66, 180–184.

Borgen, W.A., & Amundson, N.E. (1996). Strength challenge as a process for supervision. *Counselor Education and Supervision,* 36, 159-169.

Borgen, W.A., Amundson, N.E., & Harder, H.G. (1988). The experience of underemployment. *Journal of Employment Counseling*, 25, 149–159.

Borgen, W.A., Amundson, N.E., & Tench, E. (1994). *Factors that aid psychological well-being throughout the transition from adolescence to adulthood.* Unpublished manuscript, University of British Columbia.

Borgen. A.W., Pollard, D.E., Amundson, N.E., & Westwood, M.J. (1989). *Employment groups: The counselling connection.* Toronto: Lugus.

Bridges, W. (1994). *JobShift.* New York: Addison-Wesley.

Burton, M.L., & Wedemeyer, R.A. (1991). *In transition.* New York: Harper Business.

Cade, B., & O'Hanlon, W.H. (1993*). A brief guide to brief therapy.* New York: W.W. Norton.

Carlsen, M.B. (1988). *Meaning-making: Therapeutic processes in adult development.* New York: W.W. Norton.

Chanowitz, B., & Langer, E.J. (1985). Self-protection and self-inception. In M.W. Martin (Ed.), *Self deception and self understanding* (pp. 117–135). Lawrence, KS: University Press of Kansas.

Chapman, R. (1987). *American slang.* New York: Harper and Row.

Chusid, H., & Cochran, L. (1989). Meaning of career change from the perspective of family roles and dramas. *Journal of Counseling Psychology*, 36, 34–41.

Cochran, L. (1990). *The sense of vocation.* Albany, N.Y.: State University of New York.

Colaizzi, P.F. (1978) . Psychological research as the phenomenologist views it. In R.S. Valle & M. King (Eds.), *Existential-phenomenological alternatives for psychology.* New York: Oxford University Press

Combs, G., & Freedman, J. (1990). *Symbol, story & ceremony: Using metaphor in individual and family therapy.* New York: W.W. Norton.

Cooley, C.H. (1902). *Human nature and the social order.* New York: Scribner's.

Cormier, W.H., & Cormier, L.S. (1979). *Interviewing strategies for helpers: A guide to assessment, treatment and evaluation.* Monterey, CA: Brooks/Cole Publishing.

Cottone, R.R. (1992). *Theories and paradigms of counseling and psychotherapy.* Boston, MA: Allyn & Bacon.

Covey, S.R. (1989). *The 7 habits of highly effective people.* New York: Simon & Schuster.

Daniluk, J.C. (1989). The process of counseling: A spiral model. *Canadian Journal of Counselling,* 23, 329–339.

Danish, S.J., Petipas, A.J., & Hale, B.D. (1993). Life development intervention for athletes: Life skills through sports. *The Counseling Psychologist,* 21, 352–385.

Dinkmeyer, D.C., Pew, W.L., & Dinkmeyer, D.C. Jr. (1979). *Adlerian counseling and psychotherapy.* Monterey, CA: Brooks/Cole.

Dyer, W., & Vriend, J. (1975). *Counselling Techniques That Work.* Washington: APGA Press.

Dyer, W., & Vriend, J. (1973). Counselling the reluctant client. *Journal of Counseling Psychology,* 20, 3, 240–246.

Eckert, P.A. (1993). Acceleration of change: Catalysts in brief therapy. *Clinical psychology Review,* 13, 241–253.

Edelwich, J., & Brodsky, A. (1980). *Burn-out: Stages of disillusionment in the helping profession.* New York: Human Sciences Press.

Egan, G. (1982). *The skilled helper* (Second Edition). Monteray, CA: Brooks/Cole.

Eisenberg, S., & Delaney. D. (1977). *The counselling process.* Houghton Mifflin Company.

Feather, N.T., & Bond, M.J. (1983). Time structure and purposeful activity among employed and unemployed university graduates. *Journal of Occupational Psychology,* 56, 241–254.

Fineman, F. (1983). Counselling the unemployed–Help and helplessness. *British Journal of Guidance and Counselling,* 11, 1-9.

Finley, M.H., & Lee, A.T. (1981). The terminated executive: It's like dying. *Personnel and Guidance Journal,* 59, 382–384.

Fischer, C.T. (1979). Individualized assessment and phenomenological psychology. *Journal of Personality Assessment,* 43, 115–122.

Forrest, L. (1994). Career assessment for couples. *Journal of Employment Counseling,* 31, 168–186.

Freud, S. (1934). *Civilization and its discontents.* New York: Norton.

Gelatt, H.B. (1989). Positive uncertainty: A new decision-making framework for counseling. *Journal of Counseling Psychology,* 33, 252–256.

Gelatt, H.B. (1991). *Creative decision making.* Los Altos, CA: Crisp Publications.

Gelso, C.J., & Carter, J.A. (1985). The relationship in counseling and psychotherapy: Components, consequences, and theoretical antecedents. *The Counseling Psychologist,* 13 (2), 155–244.

Gilbert, D.T., & Cooper, J. (1985). Social psychological strategies of self-deception. In M.W. Martin (Ed.), *Self deception and self understanding*(pp. 75–94). Lawrence: University Press of Kansas.

Giorgi, A. (1975). An application of phenomenological methods of psychology. In A. Giorgi, C. Fischer, & E. Murray (Eds.), *Duquesne studies in phenomenological psychology* (Vol. 2). Pittsburgh: Duquesne University Press.

Glasser, W. (1965). *Reality therapy.* New York: Harper & Row.

Goffman, E. (1959). *The presentation of self in everyday life.* Garden City, N.Y.: Anchor Books.

Goldman, L. (1992). Qualitative assessment: An approach for counselors. *Journal of Counseling and Development,* 70, 616–621.

Gurney, R.M. (1980). The effects of unemployment on the psycho-social development of school-leavers. *Journal of Occupational Psychology,* 53, 205–213.

Gurney, R.M., & Taylor, K. (1981). Research on unemployment: Defects neglects and prospects. *Bulletin of the British Psychological Society,* 34, 349–352.

Haley, J. (1976*). Problem solving therapy.* San Francisco: Jossey-Bass.

Hampden-Turner, C. (1981*). Maps of the mind.* New York: Collier Books.

Haverkamp, B. (1994). Cognitive bias in the assessment phase of the counseling process. *Journal of Employment Counseling,* 31, 155–167.

Heller, F.A. (1976). Towards a practical psychology of work. *Journal of Occupational Psychology,* 49, 45–54.

Heppner, P.P., & Downing, N.E. (1982). Job interviewing for new psychologists: Riding the emotional rollercoaster. *Professional Psychology*, 13, 334–341.

Hepworth, S.J. (1980). Moderating factors of the psychological impact of unemployment. *Journal of Occupational Psychology*, 53, 139–145.

Herr, E.L. (1993). Contexts and influences on the need for personal flexibility for the 21st century (part I). *Canadian Journal of Counselling*, 27, 148–164.

Herr, E. (1993). Contexts an influences on the need for personal flexibility for the 21st century (part II). *Canadian Journal of Counselling*, 27, 219–235.

Herr, E.L., Amundson, N.E., & Borgen, W.A. (1990). Shifting economic boundaries in Europe and North America: Implications for counselling. *International Journal for the Advancement of Counselling*, 13, 295–313.

Herring, R.D. (1990). Attacking career myths among Native Americans: Implications for counseling. *The School Counselor*, 38, 13–17.

Hill, J.M.M. (1977). *The social and psychological impact of unemployment*. London: Tavistock Institute of Human Relations.

Holland, J. (1985). *The self-directed search: Professional manual.* Odessa, FL: Psychological Assessment Resources.

Jahoda, M. (1982). *Employment and unemployment: A social-psychological analysis*. Cambridge, England: Cambridge University Press.

Janoff-Bulman, R., & Frieze, I. (1983). A theoretical perspective for understanding reactions to victimization. *Journal of Social Issues*, 39, 1–17.

Kegan, R.G. (1982). *The evolving self: Problem and process in human development*. Cambridge, MA.: Harvard University Press.

Kelvin, P. (1981). Work as a source of identity: The implications of unemployment. *British Journal of Guidance and Counselling*, 9, 2–11.

Kenny, M.E. (1990). College seniors' perceptions of parental attachments: The value and stability of family ties. *Journal of College Student Development*, 31, 39–46.

Krannich, R.L. (1991). *Careering and re-careering for the 1990's.* Woodbridge, VA: Impact Publications.

Kubler-Ross, E. (1969). *On death and dying.* New York: Macmillan.

Kuhn, Lakatos, Lauden. In H.W. Reese (Ed.), *Advances in child development and behavior* (Vol. 8). New York: Academic Press.

Lakoff, G., & Johnson, M. (1980). *Metaphors we live by.* Chicago: The University of Chicago Press.

Lazarus A. (1966). Behavioural rehearsal vs. non-directive therapy vs. advice in effecting behaviour change. *Behaviour Research and Therapy*, 4, 209–212.

Loganbill, C., & Stoltenberg, C. (1983). The case conceptualization format: A training device for practicum. *Counselor Education and Supervision*, 22, 235–241.

McCall, G.H. (1987). The structure, content and dynamics of self: Continuities in the study of role identities. In K. Yardley & T. Honess (Eds.), *Self and Identity: Psychosocial Perspectives.* Toronto: John Wiley.

Maccoby, M. (1988). *Why work: Leading the new generation.* New York: Simon & Schuster.

MacDonald, D. (1993). Counselor training in Canada: An Alberta approach. *Journal of Employment Counseling*, 30, 174–184.

McKay, M., & Fanning, P. (1992). *Self esteem.* Oakland, CA: New Harbinger Publications.

Mak, A.S., Westwood, M.J., & Ishiyama, F.I. (1994). Developing role-based social competencies: A model of intercultural training for immigrants. *Journal of Career Development*, 20, 171–187.

Managers Task Group and Project Advisory Committee (1990). *My road map to EIC management.* Ottawa. Ontario. Canada Employment and Immigration Canada.

Manusov, V. (1993). "It depends on your perspective": Effects of stance and beliefs about intent on person perception. *Western Journal of Communication, 57,* 27–41.

Marsden, D. (1982). *Workless.* London: Croom Helm.

Maslow, A.E. (1968). *Toward a psychology of being* (2nd ed.). Toronto: D. Van Nostrand.

Meacham, J.A., & Emont, N.C. (1989). The interpersonal basis of everyday problem solving. In J.D. Sinnott (Ed.), *Everyday problem solving: Theory and application*. New York: Praeger.

Mead, G.H. (1934). *Mind, self and society*. Chicago: University of Chicago Press.

Melnick, J.A. (1973). Comparison of replication techniques in the modification of minimal dating behaviour. *Journal of Abnormal Psychology*, 51–59.

Myers, I.B., & McCaulley, M.H. (1985). *Manual: A guide to the development and use of the Myers-Briggs Indicator*. Palo Alto, CA: Consulting Psychologists Press.

O'Hanlon, W.H., & Weiner-Davis, M. (1989). *In search of solutions*. New York: W.W. Norton.

Orwell, G. (1975). *The road to Wigan Pier*. London: Penguin.

Paradise, L.V., & Wilder, D.H. (1979). The relationship between client reluctance and counselling effectiveness, *Journal of Occupational Psychology*, 52, 2, 240–246.

Patterson, H. (1990). Involuntary job loss. Unpublished Master's Thesis, Vancouver: University of British Columbia.

Peavy, V. (1980). Research notes on decision counselling: A paper prepared for the Occupational and Career Analysis and Devebpment Branch.

Pedersen, P. (1991). Multiculturalism as a fourth force in counseling. *Journal of Counseling and Development*, 20, 194–206.

Pedersen, P. (1993). *Culture-centered counseling skills*. New York: Homework.

Peterson, C., & Seligman, M.E.P. (1983). Learned helplessness and victimization. *Journal of Social Issues*, 39, 103–116.

Pepper, S.C. (1942). *World hypotheses: A study in evidence*. Berkley, CA: University of California Press.

Phillips, D.A., & Zimmerman, M. (1990). The developmental course of perceived competence and incompetence among competent children. In R.J. Sternberg & J. Kolligian Jr. (Eds.), *Competence considered*. New Haven: Yale University Press.

Pinkney, J.W., & Ramirez, M. (1985). Career planning myths of Chicano students. *Journal of College Student Personnel*, 26, 300–305.

300–305.

Plant, P. (1993). Unemployment and guidance: The Danish approach. *Newsletter of the International Association for Educational and Vocational Guidance*, 18, 1–2.

Riordan, et al. (1978). Helping counsellors minimize client reluctance. *Counsellor Education and Supervision*, ,12.

Rogers, C. (1961). On *becoming a person.* Boston. MA: Houghton Mifflin.

Rogoff, B., & Lave, J. (Eds.) (1984). *Everyday cognition: Its development in social context.* Cambridge, Mass.: Harvard University Press.

Rule, W.R. (1983). Family therapy and the pie metaphor. *Journal of Marital and Family Therapy*, 9, 101–103.

Rump, E.E. (1983). A comment on Dowling and O'Brien's "employed" and "unemployed" groups. *Australian Journal of Psychology*, 35, 85–90.

Sarason, S.B. (1978). The nature of problem solving in social action. *American Psychologist*, 33, 370–380.

Savickas, M.L. (1992). New directions in career assessment. In D.H. Montross and C.J. Shinkman (Eds.), *Career development: Theory and practice* (pp. 336–355). Springfield, IL: Charles C. Thomas.

Schein, E.H. (1992). Career anchors and job/role planning: The links between career planning and career development. In D.H. Montross and C.J. Shinkman (Eds.), *Career development: Theory and practice.* Springfield, IL: C.C. Thomas.

Schilling, R.F., Gilchrist, L.D., & Schinke, S.P. (1984). Coping and social support in families of developmentally disabled children. *Family Relations*, 33, 47–54.

Schlossberg, N.K., Lassalle, A., & Golec. R, (1988). *The mattering scale for adults in higher education* (6th ed.). College Park. MD: University of Maryland.

Schlossberg, N.K., Lynch, A.Q., & Chickering, A.W. (1989). *Improving higher education environments for adults.* San Francisco, CA: Jossey-Bass.

Schlossberg. N.K., & Warren. B. (1985). Growing up adult: Reactions to nontradional learning experiences. Columbia, MD: Council for Advancement of Experiential Learning.

Schon, D.A. (1983). *The reflective practitioner.* New York:

Basic Books.

Schulz, W.E. (1995). Fundamental counselling theories. Ottawa: Human Resources Development Canada.

Schumacher, E.F. (1979). *Good work*. New York: Anchor Press.

Seligman, M.E.P. (1975). *Helplessness: On depression, development and death*. San Francisco: Freeman.

Sloan, T.S. (1986). *Deciding: Self–deception in life choices*. New York: Methuen.

Stead, G.B., & Watson, M.B. (1993). The Career Myths Scale: Its validity and applicability. *International Journal for the Advancement of Counselling*, 16, 89–97.

Sterling, D.A., & Betz, N.E. (1990). Development and evaluation of a measure of fear of commitment. *Journal of Counseling Psychology*, 37, 91–97.

Stimac, M. (1977). A model for evaluation of decision passages. A facet of self-assessment. *The Personnel and Guidance Journal*, 56, 158–163.

Stone, D., & Amundson, N. (1989). Counsellor supervision: An exploratory study of the metaphoric case drawing method of case presentation in a clinical setting. *Canadian Journal of Counselling*, 23, 360–371.

Sue, W.D., & Sue, D. (1990). Barriers to effective cross-cultural counseling. In *Counseling the culturally different: Theory and practice* (2nd ed.). New York: Wiley.

Sullivan, H.S. (1953). *The interpersonal theory of psychiatry*. New York: Norton.

Super. D.E. (1957). *The psychology of careers: An introduction to vocational development*. New York: Harper.

Swinburne, P. (1981). The psychological impact of unemployment on managers and professional staff. *Journal of occupational Psychology*, 54, 47–64.

Tiggemann, M., & Winefield, M. (1984). The effects of unemployment on the mood, self-esteem, locus of control, and depressive affect of school-leavers. *Journal of Occupational Psychology*, 57, 33–42.

Toffler, A. (1970). *Future shock*. New York: Random House.

Toffler. A. (1980). *The third wave*. New York: Bantam Books.

Trompenaars, F. (1993). *Riding the waves of culture*. London:

Nicholas Brealey.

U.S. Employment Service (1979). *The General Aptitude Test Battery (GATB)*. Washington, DC: Author.

Vahamottonen, T.T.E., Keskinen, P.A., & Parrila, R.K. (1994). A conceptual framework for developing an activity-based approach to career counselling. *International Journal for the Advancement of Counselling*, 17, 19–34.

Vondracek, F.W., Lerner, R.M., & Schulenberg, J.E. (1986). *Career development: A life-span developmental approach*. London: Lawrence Edbaum Associates.

Walter, J.L., & Peller, J.E. (1992). *Becoming solution-focused in brief therapy*. New York: Brunner/Mazel.

Warr, P.B. (1983). Work, jobs and unemployment. *Bulletin of the British Psychological Society*, 36, 305–311.

Warr, P.B., Jackson, P.R., & Banks, M.H. (1982). Deviation of unemployment and psychological well being in young men and women. *Current Psychological Research*, 2, 207–214.

Westwood, M.J. (1994). Developing skills for social-cultural competencies. Unpublished manuscript. Vancouver: University of British Columbia.

Westwood, M., & Amundson, N.E. (1994). *A cross cultural workshop*. Edmonton, AB: Human Resources Development Canada.

Westwood, M., Amundson, N.E., & Borgen, W.A. (1994). *Starting points: Finding your route to employment*. Ottawa: Human Resources Development Canada.

Westwood, M.J., & Ishiyama, F.I. (1991). Challenges in counseling immigrant clients: Understanding intercultural barriers to career adjustment. *Journal of Employment Counseling*, 28, 130–143.

Young, R.A., & Collin, A. (1992). *Interpreting career: Hermeneutical studies of lives in context*. London, England: Praeger.

Young, R.E., Becker, A.L., & Pike, K.L. (1970). *Rhetoric: Discovery and change*. New York: Harcourt Brace Jovanovich.

Zawadski, B., & Lazarsfeld, P. (1935). The psychological consequences of unemployment. *Journal of Social Psychology*, 6, 244–251.